Reforming Welfare by Rewarding Work

Reforming Welfare by Rewarding Work

One State's Successful Experiment

Dave Hage

University of Minnesota Press
Minneapolis • London

MT

Published by the University of Minnesota Press
111 Third Avenue South, Suite 290
Minneapolis, MN 55401-2520
http://www.upress.umn.edu

Library of Congress Cataloging-in-Publication Data

Hage, Dave.
  Reforming welfare by rewarding work : one state's successful experiment /
Dave Hage.
      p. cm.
Includes bibliographical references and index.
  ISBN 0-8166-4094-7 (PB : alk. paper)
    1. Public welfare—Minnesota. 2. Welfare recipients—Minnesota—Case studies.
3. Welfare recipients—Employment—Minnesota—Case studies. I. Title.
HV98.M65H34 2004
362.5′09776—dc22

                                                                2003018985

Printed in the United States of America on acid-free paper

The University of Minnesota is an equal-opportunity educator and employer.

12 11 10 09 08 07 06 05 04   10 9 8 7 6 5 4 3 2 1

10/25/04

improve the well-being of poor families in ways almost never before seen. Divorce and domestic violence went down, school performance by the children went up. These gains didn't put MFIP families on a par with more affluent households, and they didn't reach every family in the program. Still, they were strong enough and unusual enough to land Minnesota a prominent place in the national welfare research literature. "For single-parent, long-term recipients—a major focus of the program and the evaluation—MFIP had strikingly consistent positive effects across a range of adult, child and family outcomes," the evaluators wrote.[7]

This book tells the story of MFIP, or rather two stories intertwined. One is a political narrative, a description of Minnesota's effort to take the meanness out of welfare politics and devise an antipoverty system built on consensus values of compassion and pragmatism. The second follows the lives of three families moving through Minnesota's new welfare-to-work system over the course of a year. It dwells on their stories in some detail, for it is the particulars of family life that best explain the complexity of poverty and the prospects for reform.

I do not mean to present Minnesota's program as a poverty cure-all. Minnesota's strategy relies heavily on the job market and it is clear, after countless experiments and studies, that some welfare recipients simply will not thrive in the workplace. Adults with mental illness, extremely low IQs, profoundly disabled children— these were the hidden welfare families, and thousands of them linger on assistance even after years of job coaching and motivational messages. Nor does MFIP cure the full ambit of social pathologies that surround poverty. As long as teenage girls bear children out of wedlock, they will face difficult lives. As long as fathers desert their families and fail to pay child support, single mothers and their children will live in economic peril. Like most states, Minnesota is trying to cure these problems too, but they are not entirely within the scope of a welfare-to-work program. Last, the version of MFIP that Minnesota uses today is not the same one that produced such exemplary results in the county field trials. The legislature trimmed the program's cash benefits and the funding for job-placement services in 1997, when the field trials ended and MFIP became a statewide program, and lawmakers made a second cut in benefits and adopted tougher application procedures in 2003, when the state faced a record budget deficit. The result is a welfare-to-work program that resembles the original in its basic design and in its results through 2002, but its overall impacts on poverty and family well-being simply have not been tested as they were during the pilot phase.

Still, Minnesota's experience offers a telling and encouraging example. It demonstrates that a state can bring civility to welfare politics and, moving beyond myth and scapegoating, construct a welfare system based on social consensus and empirical research. It shows that taxpayers will support an ambitious antipoverty strategy once they believe that poor adults are putting forth their best effort. Last, unlike many other states, Minnesota confronts the economic reality that many poor single mothers cannot give their children a decent standard of living on labor-market earnings alone. As journalist Barbara Ehrenreich demonstrated in *Nickel and Dimed*, life in low-wage America is a life of grinding struggle. Minnesota recognized this and made good on the promise that recipients would be better off working than relying on government aid. In short, it went a long way toward solving the old paradox of antipoverty policy: how to reduce hardship among poor families while encouraging them to help themselves.

Although it was conceived before the 1996 federal law known as welfare reform, the Minnesota strategy has perhaps greater significance today in the new welfare landscape created by that law. Since 1996 states have diverged sharply in their can. You will be expected to draw up an employment plan and start looking for work. MFIP has exemptions to its work requirements—for example, if you have a baby under one year or if you're caring for someone who is ill. Talk to your job counselor if you think you qualify for an exemption. But keep in mind that your five-year clock will still be ticking."

Mention of the five-year clock causes several people to look up from the paperwork before them. Two or three had been on assistance in Minnesota before 1997, when time limits took effect, and they now mutter to their neighbors that this is a big change. Anita says she has read news accounts about the controversial five-year limit and asks if there won't be some changes and extensions.

"That's possible," Brown replies. "But I want to stress that for now that is the policy in Minnesota."

The bargain that Brown is describing this afternoon sounds reasonable enough to the first-time visitor to a welfare office. But the ambitions behind it are revolutionary in the history of public assistance. Since the presidency of Richard Nixon, the nation has tried several national iterations of welfare reform and countless local experiments. Even so, the share of welfare recipients holding jobs has seldom moved above 15 percent.[1] Now Congress is asking states to push unprecedented numbers of welfare recipients into the workplace. The federal law requires that 50 percent of a state's welfare recipients be working or participating in work-preparation activities by 2002, a number that no American welfare system has ever attained. For two-parent families, the target is 90 percent.

In pursuing these goals, the new federal law brandishes the stick more than the carrot. It punishes states that fail to meet federal welfare-to-work targets, and it requires states to penalize recipients who fail to meet state welfare-to-work rules.

Minnesota has chosen to pursue the federal goals with a

combination of the carrot and the stick. It says that most clients have to find work within six months of applying for assistance or face financial penalties, and all have to engage in thirty-five hours per week of work or work-related activities, such as learning English or obtaining a high-school diploma. But it also gives them powerful rewards if they do find work: subsidized child care, wage supplements, and transportation stipends.

Brown continues, taking pains to explain that MFIP is both generous and strict. "MFIP does have education and training options, in case you want to pursue some form of schooling. But we're going to be encouraging you to move quickly toward employment, so you can go off cash assistance and have some time left on your clock if you ever need assistance in the future.

"MFIP also provides you lots of support to get you started on your work search," she continues. "The county will reimburse you for bus fare or gasoline while you're looking for work. MFIP will also help you pay for child care once you start looking for work. You may choose a licensed center or home, or if you prefer, you may use a friend or neighbor. But the county won't reimburse you if your provider isn't approved, so make sure your provider goes through the county background check and make sure they don't have any felonies."

This prompts a chuckle from Sharon, who concurs heartily. She has already arranged for the county to pay her cousin to watch her children while she goes to work, and she relates that the paperwork was substantial. "You'd better get started *yesterday* if you want it to happen any time soon," she remarks to the group.

On any given day this month a similar orientation is being conducted, with local variations, in every county across Minnesota as a new cohort of needy families enters the Minnesota Family Investment Program. In Minnesota, where welfare is administered locally, counties stand at the front line of welfare

CHAPTER 2

Reality Check (1986): A Crash Course in Poverty for a Divided Legislature

The welfare-to-work system that JoAnn Brown described to her class in the fall of 2001 seemed to embody the best of Minnesota's reputation for social compassion and political consensus. But fifteen years earlier, at the origins of the new system, the state enjoyed no such consensus on aid to needy families. In 1986 Minnesotans were waging a bitter fight over welfare, a debate that was testing the state's civic fabric and reputation for good government. Hennepin County, Minnesota's most populous county and home to a third of its welfare caseload, was receiving a steady stream of poor black families from Chicago, Gary, and other declining Rust Belt cities, which touched off a debate with ugly racial overtones. Public assistance was also a flash point in border towns such as Moorhead in northwestern Minnesota and Jackson in the south, where county commissioners insisted that the state's broad social safety net attracted poor families from the Dakotas and Iowa. Republicans insisted that poor families were exploiting the taxpayers' generosity, and politicians of both parties proposed that Minnesota should greet new poor arrivals with a one-way bus ticket home.

Much of this tension was rooted in the old welfare system,

Aid to Families with Dependent Children, or AFDC. Under this federalist hybrid, Washington paid half the cost of cash benefits and wrote broad eligibility guidelines. States paid the other half and were free to set the actual level of cash grants. Whether because of Minnesota's high cost of living (relative to that of midwestern states except Wisconsin, and relative to that of the nation, except California and the Northeast) or its progressive political tradition, the state had generally stood near the top among states in welfare benefits. In 1986 it ranked fifth nationally, paying $528 per month for a family of three, compared with $371 in neighboring North Dakota and just $118 in Alabama.[1]

This generosity had long rankled Minnesota's conservatives, and in 1986, after a long stretch out of power, they were finally in a position to do something about it. In the fall elections of 1984, Minnesota's Independent-Republicans had stunned their Democratic rivals and won a majority in the state House of Representatives. They were determined to press a new conservative agenda and to challenge the state senate, still in DFL hands, and Democratic governor Rudy Perpich. Minnesota's social-welfare system would be their battleground. In the 1985 legislative session, they had proposed deep cuts in General Assistance, a small state program that supplemented federal welfare. By 1986 they were prepared for a full-scale attack on AFDC.

Although cash welfare represented less than 2 percent of the Minnesota budget, Republican House Speaker David Jennings cited it as a symbol of profligate government and softheaded liberalism. Shortly after the legislature convened in January 1986, Representative Joel Carlson, a first-term Independent-Republican from Moorhead, introduced a bill that would cut Minnesota's monthly AFDC grant by 30 percent. The state was facing a $734 million deficit in its two-year budget cycle, and Republicans said they could save $35 million by trimming AFDC. But they also argued that cutting welfare benefits would be good social policy. Carlson, whose home district bordered North Dakota, insisted that poor families flocked to Minnesota to collect welfare. He also argued that in most counties of the state a poor adult could do better by collecting AFDC, food stamps, and government health insurance than by working full-time at a typical job. A generous AFDC grant, Carlson argued, discouraged work and undercut the American ethic of self-reliance.[2]

Carlson's proposal touched off a firestorm at the state capitol. Democrats recognized the issue's potency, given the nation's conservative drift during the Reagan era, but Governor Perpich and DFL leaders in the legislature took only a few days to decide they would fight. Perpich had opposed the previous year's plan to eliminate General Assistance, vowing famously, "I would cut off

Minnesota's reputation for generous social benefits, reflected here in an editorial cartoon from the *Nashville Tennessean,* caused alarm among the state's conservatives and prompted Republicans to propose deep cuts in welfare benefits in 1986. Cartoon by Sandy Campbell; courtesy of the *Nashville Tennessean.*

my hand before I would sign that bill," and he told emotional stories about spells of poverty during his own childhood on Minnesota's Iron Range. His Human Services commissioner, Leonard Levine, set off around the state with a team of prominent clerics, conducting news conferences to denounce the Carlson bill, and children's advocates roamed the state capitol, confronting Republicans and denouncing the young legislator from Moorhead. In mid-February, antipoverty activists organized a huge weekend rally at the capitol and a broad coalition of groups—including the League of Women Voters, the Children's Defense Fund, the GOP Feminist Caucus of Minnesota, and the National Organization for Women—announced they would oppose the Carlson bill.[3]

By mid-March, when lawmakers were supposed to be thinking about adjournment, the legislature was still deadlocked over the budget, and no issue was more intractable than AFDC. Governor Perpich was privately testing legislators on common ground for a settlement, but he warned that he would balance the state's budget himself if lawmakers could not. A conference committee representing members from the Democratic senate and the Republican house was holding marathon sessions in the capitol basement, resolving fiscal issues one by one. But negotiations ground to a halt over welfare. Then, on March 18, after a grueling and argumentative all-night session in the house, Jennings abruptly adjourned his chamber at dawn and, without any resolution of the budget crisis, sent his members home. Democrats literally trailed Jennings out of the building, shouting protests.[4]

Perpich, however, had not given up on a legislative solution. Nine days after the house walkout, he met with Jennings and Roger Moe, Democratic leader in the senate. The governor said he would call the legislature back into special session for a final budget bill, but only if the two leaders could outline a compromise in advance. As for the thorny issue of AFDC, he said, why not

Hundreds of protesters, including this young mother, rallied at the Minnesota State Capitol in early 1986 when the legislature considered a bill to cut welfare benefits by 30 percent. Photograph copyright 2002 *Star Tribune/ Minneapolis–St.Paul.*

simply set it aside? If lawmakers could agree on the rest of the budget, Perpich would appoint a bipartisan citizens commission to study the welfare question over the summer. Moe and Jennings saw a face-saving solution to their stalemate and agreed. On March 31, the two lawmakers announced they had reached a framework for a budget compromise: Perpich would call a special session, lawmakers would vote on a plan that made most of the cuts necessary to balance the state's budget, and Perpich would appoint a blue-ribbon commission to tackle the welfare controversy.

If a blue-ribbon commission appealed to all parties in March, however, it did not seem so promising two months later, when its members gathered in St. Paul for their first meeting. Perpich had allowed Moe and Jennings to nominate five members each, and as the members assembled in a conference room at the capitol, it became clear that a wide ideological gulf divided the Democrats from the Republicans. Pege Jennings, sister of the House Speaker and a social worker in southern Minnesota, said she believed that the welfare system subsidized irresponsible behavior and poor decisions by single mothers. Annie Young, a Democratic nominee and herself a former welfare recipient, replied that middle-class people had no right to judge the poor. Luanne Nyberg, another Democratic member and director of the Minnesota branch of the Children's Defense Fund, observed that the United States would have plenty of money to help poor families if only the Pentagon would sell a submarine or two. Dr. Bruce Wolff, a surgeon from the Mayo Clinic in Rochester and a member of the Republican bloc, agreed that individual members of society had an obligation to help the poor but wondered aloud why government should play any role whatsoever.[5]

The commission might have lapsed into a stubborn impasse at that first meeting, except that Moe and Jennings had nominated cochairs with unusually good political skills. Moe's nominee was

Monsignor Jerome Boxleitner, a Minneapolis priest who had built the state branch of Catholic Charities into Minnesota's biggest social-service agency. His cleric's collar brought a moral authority to his vigorous defense of the poor, but his years running food shelves and a children's home proved that he was also a highly capable executive. Boxleitner wasn't convinced that the old welfare system was such a failure, but he hoped that the commission might redirect Minnesota's poisonous welfare debate. Jennings's choice was Randy Johnson, a member of the Hennepin County Board of Commissioners from Bloomington. Johnson was a Republican in the line of Nelson Rockefeller and George Romney, a conservative who liked efficient government but believed that society had a responsibility to the poor. He also prided himself on a knack for crafting compromises, and he had done a good deal of homework on welfare-reform strategies in California, Massachusetts, and other states. He saw an opportunity for Minnesota to reinvent welfare in a way that would satisfy taxpayers while protecting the poor.

At the commission's second meeting, on June 4, when the discussion began deteriorating into another ideological quarrel, Boxleitner and Johnson stopped the argument and called for a fresh approach. They proposed that the panel spend the summer listening, not talking, and they asked the commission's staff to prepare a series of technical briefings. These would ground the commissioners in solid research and address the questions posed by Governor Perpich: Were Minnesota's grant levels excessive? Did AFDC discourage work? Did Minnesota's generous benefits attract welfare migrants from other states? What were other states doing to reduce dependency and move welfare recipients into the job market?

As it happened, the commission's staff held good credentials for the task. The staff director was Keith Ford, head of the state's

Office of Jobs Policy and a former Perpich aide who understood the political importance of a solution to the welfare impasse. His deputy was Steve Rhodes, a student of welfare-reform strategies in other states who quickly became known for his detailed memos and meeting agendas. Another deputy, Chuck Johnson, was an intern in Ford's office who had just graduated from the University of Minnesota's Humphrey Institute of Public Affairs with a master's degree in public policy. And from the Department of Human Services, the state welfare agency, came Joel Kvamme, a data wizard and Minnesota's chief authority on welfare clients and caseloads.

The decision to begin with research proved pivotal. As the staff briefings unfolded through the summer, they corrected the commissioners' misconceptions and began to sketch out common ground for reform. At the commission's June 25 meeting, a caseworker from Ramsey County outlined the household budget of a typical welfare family. She noted that monthly outlays for the bare necessities—rent ($325), food ($210), telephone and electricity ($55), laundry ($30), clothing ($30), and transportation ($30)—would more than consume the combined AFDC and food-stamps grant for a family of three, even without emergencies or the most modest family luxuries.[6] Jan Boudreneau, a caseworker from Rice County, walked commissioners through the labyrinth of paperwork that faced applicants and caseworkers alike, noting it could take as many as thirteen separate applications and fifty calculations to enroll one family on AFDC, Medical Assistance, and food stamps. Later, state demographer Tom Gillaspy addressed the question of welfare migration, noting that despite its generous benefits package, Minnesota lost about as many poor people every year as it gained.[7]

As the summer went on, the commissioners broadened their scope. They learned that almost 90 percent of adult AFDC recipients were single mothers, and that about 80 percent received no financial support from the fathers of their children. They learned that many AFDC recipients asked for job training, but that AFDC was full of financial penalties for clients who actually found work. They heard that many AFDC mothers were enrolled in community colleges and vocational-technical schools, but that they often lost a portion of their food stamps if they received government loans for tuition or books.[8] They also began to understand the crucial economics of child care. The typical welfare recipient in Minnesota had two children, at least one preschooler and often two. This meant that she would pay anywhere from $400 to $900 per month for child care if she went to work. Yet with her skills and work experience, she could expect to earn about $6 per hour, or $960 per month if she could find full-time work. In other words, after paying for child care, she could have less money working than she would have staying home with her children and collecting welfare. Worse, she would probably lose her right to free health insurance, since the government's Medicaid program was tethered to AFDC and generally did not extend to the working poor.

But it was on August 6, when Joel Kvamme briefed the commission on welfare caseloads and the job market, that commissioners achieved their first breakthrough. Kvamme was already something of a legend within the Department of Human Services, both as the agency's top theoretician on questions of poverty and as the author of a series of research papers on what was called welfare dynamics. Kvamme had come to Minnesota after a stint working for the U.S. Department of Health, Education, and Welfare in Chicago, but he brought more than a bureaucrat's credentials: he held a master's degree in social science from the University of Chicago, and during a sabbatical in graduate school had gone to work as a front-line welfare worker in Cook County,

Illinois. But he was also the son of a Lutheran minister who had served a series of small towns in the Upper Midwest, and he was unusually thoughtful about moral behavior and society's obligations to the poor.

As the furor over welfare and dependency crescendoed in the mid-1980s, Kvamme had begun to ask himself what the government actually knew about welfare families. The answer, he decided, was not much. Although most states had "snapshot" data about families on public assistance at any given time, they knew little about these families as they passed through the system. What crises caused poor, single mothers to apply for government assistance? How long did they stay on welfare? Where were the fathers of their children? What enabled them to leave welfare again? Were they better off after they left? Although two researchers at Harvard University, David Ellwood and Mary Jo Bane, had begun to study these questions, most welfare administrators in most states had little grasp of the answers.

Poring over computer printouts and financial reports at Human Services headquarters, a converted warehouse on Lafayette Road near downtown St. Paul, Kvamme realized he would have to construct his own data set to answer these questions, and in 1985 he had asked his superiors for a special assignment to do just that. The resulting reports, known as longitudinal studies because they tracked welfare families over time, had created quite a stir within state government one year earlier, and Kvamme now laid his findings before the commission.

It turned out that Minnesota's welfare recipients were not a homogenous group, and certainly weren't the urban welfare queens of popular stereotype. There were college graduates and high-school dropouts. There were single mothers with one child and married couples with huge families. A large share of the adult recipients were unwed mothers, but the majority had been

Joel Kvamme, a statistics and operations expert at the Minnesota Department of Human Services, provided crucial research for the 1986 Welfare Reform Commission and later led the team that would design Minnesota's new welfare system. Photograph courtesy of Katie Bauer, Minnesota Department of Human Services.

married and were now divorced or separated. Many of the recipients had substantial work experience and knew exactly what sort of job would get them back on their feet. Others were essentially strangers to the job market. They had married early and stayed home with young children; they came onto assistance when abandoned by a husband, and they were more likely to leave welfare by finding a new breadwinner than by finding a job.[9]

Drawing on his days as a Cook County welfare worker, Kvamme also asked whether the welfare system gave its clients any incentive to leave public assistance. Most of the adults he studied had worked in the past, but most had only the most meager skills and earnings prospects. Of those who had worked, more than a quarter had held jobs in food service—an industry notorious for low wages and part-time hours—and many others had worked in low-paying custodial or clerical jobs. At these wages, after paying for child care and transportation, the parents would actually lose money by leaving welfare for work.

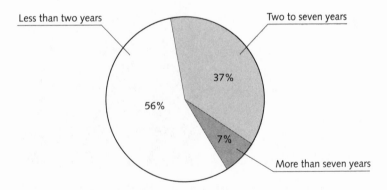

Duration of recipients' welfare use in Minnesota under Aid to Families with Dependent Children. Joel Kvamme's most striking finding, shown here in a pie chart, revealed that long-term dependency was relatively rare among welfare clients in Minnesota in the late 1970s and early 1980s.

workers, local politicians. So in late September Steve Rhodes drafted a "laundry list" of 126 policy options, from welfare time limits to public jobs to pregnancy prevention, and scheduled six field hearings at cities around the state.

Testimony at the field hearings was voluminous and lively, and it would move both wings of the commission further toward the middle. At a hearing in Winona on October 8, the commissioners heard from a registered nurse who wanted to go back to school for a theater degree and thought that AFDC should support her in graduate school. Randy Johnson remembered thinking that this was a bit much, that it was unfair to ask taxpayers to support the graduate-school career of someone who already had one degree and a good job. Much to his surprise, the Reverend Boxleitner leaned over and whispered the same sentiment.[17] At a later hearing in St. Paul, the commission heard from a woman who had applied for welfare in the 1960s after her husband left her and their four children. Using AFDC to pay rent and government grants to cover tuition, she had completed a college degree—Phi Beta Kappa—and gone on to a career in social work. She told the commission, "You eat a lot of macaroni and cheese on an AFDC budget." But she estimated that since leaving assistance she had paid ten times more in taxes than she had received in government aid.[18] Bruce Wolff remembered such testimony as an epiphany and concluded that many AFDC recipients were exemplary citizens who made a legitimate case for government aid.

Mostly, however, the witnesses confirmed with anecdotal testimony the commissioners' conviction that AFDC was too complicated and too punitive:

> We went on AFDC when the car I was driving was repossessed and the major appliances my ex-husband and I bought while we were married had been sold off to pay for living expenses. While I was

selling my things and the car was being repossessed, a $1,000 guaranteed student loan had become delinquent. I am now faced with not completing the three quarters (of college) I have left because of new government regulations. I'm not here, though, to talk about education. I am here to talk about desperately needed child-care funding. If there was any one thing that interfered with our getting off welfare it was having to pay for my own daycare expenses. That, combined with the cost of transportation to daycare and school in the winter, set my school plans back two quarters.

—Caryl Rau, October 14, Detroit Lakes

After two years of receiving aid, I have decided to go back to school, but I find I am penalized for doing so. My rent is increased and my food stamps are taken away because my grants and loans are considered income. All I ask for is a chance to get an education.

—Debra Keckhafer, October 8, Winona

My ex-husband has abandoned me and our children economically, leaving me to deal with the total support and welfare of our children. Why is it that society confronts my use of AFDC and not my ex-husband's lack of responsibility?

—Kathleen Hill, October 22, Minneapolis

In January 1986, my then-16-year-old daughter gave birth to a child. I called Washington County to ask about medical coverage for the baby, but was turned down because I am employed. So I called the state welfare office and was told that if I quit my job I could receive medical assistance for the baby and my three kids and I wouldn't have to seek employment for five years. I can't believe this. Where is the incentive to be self-supportive?

—Beverly Friendt, October 10, Duluth

Let's talk about economic realities. My monthly grant is $437. My rent is $335 a month. That buys us a one-bedroom apartment in a not-so-nice neighborhood. No yard. From where I stand, luxury looks like a two-bedroom apartment.

—Margaret Kaiser, October 22, St. Paul[19]

By the time field hearings concluded in late October, the commissioners could glimpse consensus on core principles for reform. They agreed that AFDC actually discouraged work and demeaned its clients. They agreed that welfare should furnish temporary aid, not permanent support, in most cases. They concluded that most welfare recipients preferred work to the dole and would seek jobs if they saw that their families would be better off. They agreed that the state should provide work supports such as child care and health insurance, but that in return the government should require most welfare recipients to seek work or work-related training.[20]

But they hadn't quite achieved harmony. Democrats on the panel noted that child-care subsidies and public health insurance would be expensive, and they argued that the commission should recommend a higher level of state spending to make welfare reform succeed. The Republicans objected, noting that Governor Perpich had explicitly ordered the commission not to recommend big new government programs.[21] After one tense meeting in November, Randy Johnson actually called Perpich's chief of staff and asked that the governor give the Democrats a talking-to. The next week, fearing that the commission might fall into disarray, Jerome Boxleitner and Johnson decided it was time to draft consensus recommendations where consensus existed. They asked Luanne Nyberg and Pege Jennings, who seemed to be the sharpest members of their respective blocs, to go off together and write a draft report. After incorporating a series of revisions and consulting the other commissioners, Boxleitner and Johnson wrote a preface that articulated the priest's concerns for the dignity of families and the politician's emphasis on responsible spending.

In the third week of November, Keith Ford briefed Perpich on the commission's conclusions, and on November 25, 1986, Boxleitner and Johnson released their report to the public. It showed how much the commissioners had learned during seven months of work and how far the commission's hawks and doves had moved toward middle ground. Echoing Kvamme's research, the report concluded that AFDC "works as intended" for the majority of clients but said that the system had failed a small and costly group of families who lingered on assistance for years. In its discussion of poor families, the commission was remarkably sympathetic. "Most recipients see the system as temporary and not an end in itself," the introduction read. "They want a job and economic viability just like everyone else." In its description of the AFDC bureaucracy, however, the report was unstintingly harsh. "The welfare system assumes the worst and too often gets the worst as a result," it read. "The system focuses too much of its efforts on eligibility, fraud and abuse, rather than helping those who need help to secure a sound future for themselves and their families."[22]

Much to the surprise of the early skeptics, the commissioners not only achieved consensus on broad principles, they laid out several proposals for reform. They specifically renounced any cut in Minnesota's AFDC grant, though they proposed restructuring benefits to make sure the system would reward work. They said that counties should offer intensive "case management," that is, close supervision by caseworkers, to the small number of clients who were at risk for long-term dependency—chiefly those without a high-school diploma and those who had borne children out of wedlock. And they said the state should subsidize child care and medical insurance for the working poor, lest those expenses overwhelm them and throw them back on AFDC.

In scope, the report was wildly ambitious. It called on the federal government to waive nearly a dozen major regulations so that Minnesota could experiment with work incentives, and it blithely recommended changes that would rewrite the job descriptions of thousands of state and county employees working in job counseling, health care, welfare administration, and higher education.

But the commission also accomplished something that almost no one expected at the outset. It sketched out a tough-minded, research-based middle ground for reform. It concluded that most of the young single mothers on welfare could and should work, a controversial proposition at the time. It argued that society had a right to insist that welfare recipients improve their own prospects. But it also asserted that most welfare recipients were responsible citizens who would seek jobs and improve their lives if the system gave them the right incentives. And it argued that true welfare reform would require generous new programs to subsidize child care, health insurance, and transportation—benefits that most middle-class workers take for granted. All these conclusions, so obvious today, were startling assertions that would transform the welfare debate in Minnesota and lay the groundwork for dramatic reforms.

CHAPTER 3

Real Life, Fall 2001

Patty slides into a booth at the Perkins restaurant in Coon Rapids, lights a Marlboro, and begins recounting her latest battle with authority. "The school district, in all its wisdom, won't let my daughter ride the school bus anymore." She pours hot water over a tea bag. "Budget cuts. Any kid who lives less than a mile from school has to walk."

It's our first face-to-face interview, but Patty is wasting no time with pleasantries. She's irate. She lives a mile away, on a stretch of road in the middle of the sprawling Anoka-Hennepin School District, and now her eight-year-old daughter, Samantha, will have a twenty-minute walk to school. "Oh, she could still ride the bus," Patty continues. "It's just that now I have to pay for it. Slick way for them to raise revenue."

The anecdote is typical of Patty, as I will learn in coming months. She's a funny blend of brassy party girl and protective mother. Today she looks more the party girl: petite black engineer boots, blue jeans, a V-neck lavender pullover, and a black leather jacket. Her long auburn hair is pulled back in a ponytail that recalls Olivia Newton-John in *Grease*. She looks much younger than thirty-eight, though her throaty cough betrays years of hard living.

I met Patty at a Minnesota Family Investment Program orientation in Anoka County, when she first applied for county aid in late 2001. She resembles many of the hard-luck, blue-collar parents who were applying for public assistance in this north suburban community. She was born in Texas but grew up mostly in the inner-ring suburbs of Minneapolis, communities that were tidy and prosperous in 1950 but growing a bit seedy by the time Patty was growing up in the 1970s. She was bright in school but had little patience for homework and spent most of her time with pals, cruising the suburban strips in the first muscle car she could buy on earnings from baby-sitting and waitressing.

Patty was astute enough to take a series of clerical and business classes in high school, but during her senior year she met a rambunctious mechanic named Mike, who had a way with girls as well as carburetors. She gave up any thought of college and moved in with him shortly after graduation. They never talked about marriage, but for a dozen years they had a lot of fun. They set up living near Elk River, on the fringe of the Twin Cities suburbs. She worked as a bookkeeper and, occasionally, as a bartender. He fixed cars. It wasn't upward mobility, but it kept them in cigarettes and Pontiacs.

For a long time Patty didn't think about having children. Her own childhood had been so-so. Her mother was loving but bossy and distracted; her stepfather was leering and mean. But as she approached her thirties, she began to want a daughter and to believe that she could do a better job of bringing up a little girl.

Having a child with Mike, however, was problematic. Their life revolved around taverns and parties. Worse, Mike had a mean streak. To Patty, a night at the bar was a social occasion. To him, it seemed to be revenge for a bitter life. He would get drunk and start swearing at her. Then he would get drunker and hit her. But on the day that Patty told him she was pregnant, she reckoned things would work out. "He said he felt like he had just won the lottery. He thought it was the greatest thing that had ever happened."

The two made a deal. When the baby came, Mike would keep working full-time but Patty would cut back her hours, perhaps go back to part-time bartending. She insisted on being a mostly stay-at-home mom, at least while her daughter was young.

Samantha was scarcely six months old when the agreement started to break down. Mike had two businesses, one fixing cars and one plowing snow, and neither was prospering. He groused that Patty wasn't bringing in much money. He complained about the baby's crying, especially when he was trying to sleep off a hangover. Perhaps worse, Patty wasn't available to go barhopping with him on short notice. He would go off alone, sometimes for two or three days at a time, then come back in a foul mood.

For a time, Patty put up with it. She thought life would improve when Samantha was a little older and didn't cry as much, that Mike would appreciate a little girl who walked and talked more than an infant who needed constant attention. She told him that her life was no picnic, staying home and up half the night with a demanding baby. Mike sneered.

By the time Samantha reached her first birthday, life in their house had gotten downright scary. One Sunday afternoon Mike came home with a pal to watch football on television. When Patty sassed off to his friend, Mike grabbed her by the wrist and pulled so hard that he broke a bone. Another day he grabbed Samantha from her arms and punched Patty so hard that he hit the baby on his backswing. The days when he disappeared to go drinking were the peaceful ones, except that they were filled with dread about when he might return.

"He would always call when he was on his way home. He

would be coming down or hungover and really ugly. He'd tell me how hard he was going to hit me when he got home.

"So one night, after I get one of these calls from him, I called 911. They said, 'Ma'am, it's his house and you had better leave.' I said, 'Great. It's ten below zero and my car hasn't started for a week. What am I supposed to do for transportation, hook up the dog to my daughter's sled?'"

As Patty recounts the evening, Mike was angry when he got home. He raged around the house and tore the phone from the wall. Then he passed out on the bed. Patty gathered up the baby and, without bothering to put on boots, made her way outside to the car. She was opening the car door when he grabbed her from behind, dragged her back into the house, and knocked her to the floor. When he passed out again, Patty wired the phone back to the wall and called the police. She spent the night with a girlfriend and pressed charges the next morning. "I was not going to let him touch me again, and I was not going to have my daughter grow up thinking that it was OK for men to hit women."

Patty's ordeal with Mike was horrifying, but not unusual among women who wind up on welfare. Surveys conducted in the mid-1990s found that 15 to 30 percent of mothers on public assistance had been victims of domestic abuse,[1] and welfare job counselors could relate story after story of clients showing up for interviews with black eyes and bruised ribs. That sort of violence was doubly or triply pernicious: it forced young mothers to set off on their own, even if they had no money or nearby relatives, and it often produced emotional scars that left them jittery and unpredictable in the workplace.

Patty never doubted her decision to leave, but she quickly discovered that life as a single mother in a remote Twin Cities exurb was no fun. She found an apartment, went back to part-time bartending, and found a neighborhood teenager who would watch Samantha while she went to work.

Patty thought of herself as a responsible parent for leaving a violent boyfriend and starting over with her daughter. But that didn't make her a saint. One night, when Samantha was three, Patty stayed at the bar after her shift and had a few rounds with her friends. She was well past the legal limit when she walked out and, sure enough, a county sheriff's deputy stopped her on the way home. At her court hearing for driving while intoxicated she asked the judge to consider the difficulties of a single mother. She warned that if he gave her jail time, Samantha would have to stay with her father, a drunk and a lout. The judge was not convinced and gave Patty thirty days in the county jail. The experience left Patty angry with the court system but she tried to behave, obeying the rules and scrubbing squad cars as a sign of good behavior. When she was released after fifteen days, she picked up Samantha at Mike's house and resolved to lead a cleaner life.

Life as a single mother worked for a time, until Patty got crosswise with the night manager and quit her bartending job. By now, she had had enough of Elk River. It had presented a certain cowboy charm while she and Mike were together. But viewed through the eyes of a single parent with few friends, living in a rundown apartment complex, it lost much of its appeal. The inner suburbs of the Twin Cities seemed more like home to her and a more likely place to find work. In the fall of 2000, she took a factory job not far from Elk River and began thinking about a move.

A year later, when Samantha was six, Patty met a new guy through a girlfriend in Coon Rapids. He ran a drywall business in the nearby suburb of Fridley, coached youth baseball, and seemed to like her. She had no friends left in Elk River and decided it was time to move closer to the Twin Cities. So, in October 2001, Patty packed up Samantha and herself in Ethyl, her reliable 1988 pickup truck, and made the twenty-mile move to an apartment in Coon Rapids.

That was the weekend when everything fell apart. Dear old Ethyl blew a piston ring during the move and, after one hundred and thirty thousand miles, was destined for the junkyard. Patty tore a shoulder tendon carrying boxes and called her supervisor to say she would need some time off. He told her she was fired.

"There I was. No car, no job, about to get evicted. Christmas two months away. I said, 'OK, that's it. I surrender.'"

A week later she went to the Anoka County Human Services building in Blaine and applied for welfare.

A cold drizzle is falling in the parking lot of Huntington Place as Lucille arrives home in a cab from grocery shopping. She pays the driver and then struggles to lift her grocery bags from the backseat. At five foot one inch and 240 pounds she's a little ungainly, and a back injury from one of her many factory jobs makes her wince when she lifts heavy objects. Still, she does not look like a woman old enough to have two teenaged daughters. Her face is round, unwrinkled, and mahogany brown, and a slight natural pout gives her an almost girlish look, even at age thirty-one.

Huntington Place has been home to Lucille and her daughters for three years, though she is not happy about it. The apartment complex consists of six drab brick buildings laid out across an expanse of parking lots. It was built in the sterile style of 1960s suburbia for young couples on their way up in the suburban blush of the postwar era. But the prosperous young couples moved on before long, and this part of Brooklyn Park, showing its age and offering modest apartments, has turned into a neighborhood for low-income immigrant and African American families who want something safer and cheaper than the rental neighborhoods of Minneapolis.

Two morose security guards patrol the grounds, motoring slowly through the parking lots, and three boys in gangsta dress are seeking shelter in Lucille's lobby as she enters. She suspects them of dealing drugs and, though she has no proof, she could be right. Brooklyn Park police were called to Huntington Place an average of fifteen times every week during 2001, often for drug-related complaints,[2] and during the previous summer a resident was shot during a parking-lot altercation at 2:00 A.M. When it gets loud outside—party music or neighbors hollering at each other—Lucille shuts her kitchen window and tells her daughters to stay inside. "I can't be bothered with that foolishness," she says with a little waft of one hand.

It's not an ideal place to raise children, but it's where Lucille wound up after a not-quite-successful migration north from the Deep South. She was born in 1970 in a tiny village in the Mississippi Delta. Her mother had divorced young and wound up on AFDC with five children. Lucille, the youngest of the family, was serious and persistent, but she struggled in school and had to repeat grades seven and nine. Still, she resolved to finish high school and pursue a nursing degree. These ambitions received one setback the year that Lucille turned sixteen and found herself pregnant after a one-night fling with a local boy. They received a second setback one day in school six months later. She was sitting in class doing a math problem when she looked down to see a boy in her class trying to look up her dress. Not one to suffer fools, she kicked him in the face. The school principal was not amused and gave her a choice: five days' suspension or five licks from the reed he kept in his office.

"I wasn't a child," Lucille recalls. "I was about to have my first baby. I wasn't going to take no whupping." So she took the suspension, went home, and stewed over the injustice of her circumstances, and never returned to school.

After the baby came, Lucille started working at a local community center, serving food and helping the elderly with recreational activities. Before long she had a new boyfriend, but when she became pregnant with his child, he disappeared. This was the 1980s, when birth-control devices were widely available in the United States and many sexually active teenagers were using the pill or condoms. It wasn't until years later that anyone would give Lucille an IQ test and discover that, like many adults with low intelligence, she had trouble with even modest precautions and simple short-term planning. She continued living with her mother, who watched the babies while Lucille went off to work at the community center.

Then one day in 1992 her sister called from Minnesota. She had been in Minneapolis for fifteen years and had held a series of good jobs as a personal-care attendant. Nursing homes in Minnesota were desperate for staff, her sister said, and would pay far more than the $4.25 Lucille was earning at the community center in Mississippi. Lucille thought it over for a year and discussed it with her new boyfriend. The two were happy together and game to make the move. They married in 1993 and one year later went north to Minnesota.

At first, their move had all the hallmarks of success. Minnesota's unemployment rate was the lowest in the nation, and employers of every stripe were desperate for help. Minneapolis schools, though far from perfect, were a big improvement over those in Mississippi. With her older daughter in grade school and her younger one about to enter kindergarten, Lucille figured the family's prospects were bright.

But Lucille and her husband struggled from the first. He too was a high-school dropout and never got much further than a series of car-wash jobs. She landed a job at a Taco Bell, then moved on to a series of factory jobs that never quite panned out. She worked for a while in a diet-candy factory, but the chemical ingredients gave her headaches, so she quit. Then she took a job in a perfume factory, but the fumes were even worse. She worked for a time at a small printing plant, feeding paper into printing presses, but before long the constant bending and lifting gave her a back injury. The family was on and off public assistance, depending on his earnings at the car wash and whether she was between jobs. Then in 2000 Lucille landed the best job she'd ever had: packaging water filters at a PUR Water Purifications Company plant in Brooklyn Park. It was steady work at forty hours per week, and it paid $9.75 an hour plus health insurance and two weeks of vacation every year. Finally, she thought, the move north was paying off. It was not to last. Minnesota's economy began softening some months before the disaster of September 11, and in the spring of 2001 Lucille got a layoff notice. Four months later, after months of arguments over bills and children, her husband left. Broke and alone with her daughters, she went back on assistance, this time enrolling in MFIP.

As a black woman from the Deep South living in suburban Minnesota, Lucille feels a bit of an outcast, and she understands that public attitudes toward welfare are freighted with racial overtones. African Americans are not, as many people think, a majority of welfare recipients in Minnesota or most other states. But they are overrepresented on the welfare rolls—about 30 percent of the MFIP caseload as against less than 5 percent of the general population—and they populate many of the worst stereotypes about welfare.[3]

Race was never far below the surface in Minnesota's welfare debates, with white conservatives arguing that generous benefits attracted "outsiders" to the state and social liberals arguing that

black poverty was a legacy of decades of legal and illegal discrimination. But whether discrimination played a role in Lucille's long
struggle is a complicated question. Any number of "audits" conducted by civil-rights groups and government enforcement agencies—sending black and white candidates to apply for the same
job or the same apartment—have proven the presence of racial
discrimination in the American workplace and housing market. A
survey by the Urban Coalition of St. Paul found that low-income
people of color were more likely than their white counterparts
to rely on public transportation and to live in neighborhoods of
concentrated poverty, two more barriers to employment. And in a
survey of recipients approaching their five-year time limits in
2002, the Minnesota Department of Human Services found that
half said they had been the victims of racial or ethnic discrimination.[4] Even among MFIP job counselors, the question was controversial. Some insisted that a black client and a white client,
with comparable qualifications and characteristics, could find jobs
with equal ease in the Twin Cities, while others argued that black
clients would always have to work harder and prepare longer than
their white counterparts.

For her part, Lucille says she has seldom felt actual prejudice
in her own life. "Once," she says in the clipped and guarded tone
that characterizes her sentences. "When my husband and I were
visiting friends in Alabama. We came out of a store, and some
white man passed us by and said, 'Why don't you go back where
you came from?' I told my husband to ignore that. There's no
dealing with ignorant people.

"But discrimination, no. Where I came from, white people
and black people all had the same jobs."

Still, Lucille wonders how her life might have turned out
differently if she were not the descendent of slaves and sharecrop-
pers who worked in the deepest disadvantage of the rural South.

"You wonder sometimes," she says, smoothing out a wrinkle in her skirt. "You do wonder."

These days, stuck in a dreary suburban neighborhood with two daughters growing up rapidly, Lucille spends more time reflecting on her choices than on her race. Dropping out of high school. Two babies with two different men. A quick marriage that eventually failed. "Some days," she says, "you know, I wish I'd taken that whupping."

At the MFIP orientation where I first met her, Meg seemed a bit out of place. She took notes studiously and seemed more engaged, more *impatient* than the other applicants in the room. Indeed, as she laid out her story, she seemed not quite to have accepted that she was part of the welfare system or to have comprehended the long, slow-motion disaster that brought her to public assistance in the first place. She grew up on St. Paul's South Side and later in the suburbs northeast of the city. Her mother worked for the Minnesota highway department and her stepfather sold medical equipment. Meg is of German and Ojibwe descent, but her mouse-brown hair and pale complexion look more European than Native American, and although she occasionally wears T-shirts decorated with Ojibwe designs, she always identified with middle-class suburbia more than with the Twin Cities Indian community. When she graduated from White Bear Lake High School in 1991 she enrolled at the University of Minnesota, intending to prepare for medical school. "My stepfather had a friend who was a surgeon. I had visited his clinic once or twice and I thought, yeah, that's what I want."

But in her second year at the university, while working in a campus cafeteria, she met a foreign exchange student named Anthony who was visiting from Brazil. He was charming, handsome, and self-confident, and they quickly became an item.

Anthony had traditional ideas about romance and family, and after they had dated for a year, they were married in the spring of 1993. Meg got pregnant immediately. When the baby boy arrived, she dropped out of school. She didn't think of it as a setback or a mistake; she was blissfully in love and happy to be a mother. A year later, she was back in school, this time training to be a laboratory assistant. But Anthony wanted a big family, and in 1997 Meg got pregnant again.

This time Anthony encouraged her to stay home for a while with the babies. He had since graduated, received a green card to stay in the United States, and was starting a small business as a broker of computer components. Meg was happy enough with the life of a stay-at-home mom; she took more pleasure than she had expected in the rewards and surprises of small children. But before long the couple was under stress. Anthony now insisted that Meg stay home with the babies and let him provide for the family. Meg saw that his business wasn't bringing in enough money to pay the family's bills. "But when I brought that up, he thought I was criticizing him. He said I was mean."

They eventually agreed that Meg could work part-time, and she quickly found a job in the office of a Minneapolis hotel. It was a far cry from the medical career she had aspired to, but the hours were good and the clerical work was interesting. Then in the fall of 2000, Meg became pregnant with their third baby and the old tensions burst to the surface again. Anthony wanted her to stay home. She said they couldn't afford it. He took it as criticism of his business skills, flew into a rage, and walked out. They were divorced a month later.

Meg responded with a characteristic blend of testiness and pride. "I said, 'I can handle this. I can do this on my own.'" With help from her brother and her mother, who now lived in St. Paul, she found an inexpensive apartment on the East Side. She enrolled

Zachary at one of the best elementary schools in the St. Paul school district and found a less expensive child-care center for Samuel. At work, she asked for longer hours and a raise, and got both.

When she gave birth in July 2001, this time to a baby girl, Meg planned to take a three-month maternity leave, but still thought her plans would work out. She was exhausted from raising two boys while caring for an infant, but her mother watched the children several days a week, and Meg had set aside some savings to tide her over. But she hadn't foreseen the events of September 11. In late September she called her boss at the hotel to discuss a return date to work. He sighed and told her what had happened to the travel industry since the World Trade Center tragedy. He said it was unlikely that he would have a job for her at the end of her leave in October. Two weeks later, the hotel simply closed the office where she had worked, and she was out of a job for good.

Still, Meg did not surrender. She drew down her savings to make her November rent payment, then borrowed $500 from her mother and started poring over the want ads. By mid-November she hadn't found a job. She borrowed more money from her brother, and then another $500 from her stepfather. "He said, 'I told you not to go into the travel business.'"

On December 1, having struck out with the want ads and tapped out her relatives, she went to the Ramsey County building in downtown St. Paul and applied for MFIP. Meg fidgets as she tells this part of the story and her eyes turn to the boys. "Zachary, stop harassing your brother," she says with gentle exasperation. Applying for welfare absolutely galled her, but it was the only rational step she could think of.

Through a winter of chaotic days and fitful nights, Meg managed to keep a surprising equanimity. One day a few months after the divorce, Anthony stopped by with some presents for the boys and took them on an outing for the day. "He said that's the first time he understood how hard it was to be a single parent," Meg remembered later. "He said, 'You know, you're really a remarkable woman. I probably never said that before.' I said, 'Yeah, well, determination can do a lot.'"

CHAPTER 4

Remaking Welfare (1987–1994): Making Work Pay

When Minnesota's welfare-reform commission went out of business in late 1986, Governor Rudy Perpich told colleagues he was delighted with its work. By ruling out any cut in Minnesota's basic welfare grant, the commission had vindicated Perpich's decision to defend AFDC in the legislature one year earlier. Yet by proposing a new social contract between the state and welfare recipients, the commission had delivered a pragmatic antipoverty strategy that Perpich could sell to lawmakers of both parties and to a broad swath of voters.

In January 1987, the Perpich administration began drafting legislation that would move Minnesota in the direction laid out by the commission's cochairs, Reverend Jerome Boxleitner and Randy Johnson. The bill created Priority Access to Human Services (PATHS), a job-readiness program for welfare recipients who volunteered to seek work. It subsidized child care for welfare parents who went to school at state colleges and vocational-technical schools. And it funded intensive "case management"— job counseling, family therapy, drug treatment, and so forth—for a small number of recipients who seemed incapable of putting their lives in order.[1]

The PATHS bill got a warm reception at the legislature, where the political climate had changed dramatically since the bitter 1986 session. Democrats had spent the summer depicting state Republicans as mean-spirited extremists and the DFL had run up large gains in the November elections. Democrats had recaptured control of the Minnesota house and retained control of the state senate, while Perpich trounced his Republican rival, a family-values conservative named Cal Ludeman. As a practical matter, this meant that Democrats could pass almost any legislation Perpich sent them. As a political matter, it meant less welfare-bashing at the state capitol. Republicans seemed chastened

Minnesota governor Rudy Perpich was delighted with the work of his welfare-reform commission, which resolved the partisan fight over public assistance and proposed a new social contract between the state and the poor. Shown with Perpich are (from left) Annie Young, Jack Jones, Representative Ann Wynia, Senator Marilyn Lantry, Norm Bruegmann, Senator Linda Berglin, Keith Ford, Luanne Nyberg, Jobs and Training commissioner Joe Samargia, and Pat Fredley. Young, Jones, Bruegmann, Nyberg, and Fredley were members of Perpich's commission; Ford was its staff director. Photograph courtesy of Luanne Nyberg.

by their November defeat, and conservative Democrats, who often voted with Republicans on welfare legislation, fell back into line now that compassion had proved to be a winning issue.

In the House of Representatives, Lee Greenfield, the dean of Minneapolis Democrats on social policy, carried the Perpich bill and expanded its child-care and case-management provisions. In the senate, Republican minority leader Duane Benson said his party would actually increase the funding for child care and health insurance. Where lawmakers faulted the bill, they said it didn't go far enough; the state still faced a substantial budget deficit and the Perpich administration hadn't found the money for a big jobs program or a major training initiative. In May, just a year after the nasty fight over Representative Joel Carlson's proposal to slash welfare benefits, both houses passed a bill that would add $24 million annually to spending on needy families.

Still, the PATHS bill was only a placeholder toward fundamental welfare reform. County welfare directors soon complained they couldn't hire enough social workers at the bill's funding levels to reach all of their troubled families. The bill's modest child-care subsidies were quickly oversubscribed by welfare parents returning to school. And the law created no comprehensive new health-insurance plan for poor families entering the low-wage job market. Luanne Nyberg, the Children's Defense Fund director who had helped bring Minnesota liberals onboard for an overhaul of welfare, accused the Perpich administration of abandoning genuine reform.

But perhaps the biggest obstacle to fundamental reform was the web of federal regulations that governed antipoverty programs. The rules of AFDC, for example, said that any welfare recipient who found a job would, after a four-month grace period, lose essentially a dollar of benefits for every dollar of wages. If Minnesota wanted welfare families to see significant rewards for working, it would need an exemption from that rule. Federal rules governing AFDC and food stamps also imposed strict asset tests; a family with one used car could find itself ineligible for aid. If Minnesota expected welfare recipients to get to work in the state's harsh winters and far-flung rural counties, it would have to let them own reliable cars. Last, the Perpich administration wanted to consolidate several federal assistance programs to cut paperwork for confused clients and overworked county caseworkers. The careful research reports produced by Joel Kvamme showed that some 80 percent of families who received AFDC also received food stamps. Yet the two programs had separate application forms, separate compliance rules, and conflicting eligibility thresholds. Merging them into one, simplifying the process for families and caseworkers alike, would require special federal permission.

Before the legislature adjourned in the spring of 1987, Perpich summoned his new Human Services commissioner, Sandra Gardebring, and asked why Minnesota couldn't obtain federal "waivers" to experiment with welfare as other states were. Perpich was a governor who studied other states and liked to think of Minnesota as a pioneer. He could see that welfare reform was on the move nationally. He was active in the National Governors Association, whose chair that year, Arkansas governor Bill Clinton, was agitating for welfare reform in state legislatures. President Ronald Reagan had, in his state of the union address in January, called on Congress to overhaul welfare and had encouraged governors to begin experiments of their own. And just across the border in Wisconsin, a new governor named Tommy Thompson had promised a radical series of experiments in family responsibility. Returning from Perpich's office that day, Gardebring gathered her own deputies and described a new mandate from the governor: pretend that federal regulations don't exist and design the ideal welfare system from scratch.

That spring, at the Office of Jobs Policy, Keith Ford re-assembled the staff that had worked for the welfare-reform commission. Steve Rhodes began looking at welfare-to-work experiments in California, Massachusetts, Maine, and Wisconsin. Chuck Johnson started working with counties on implementation of the new PATHS employment system. Ford himself wrote to Charles Hobbs, a Reagan adviser who ran a special White House task force on state-level welfare innovation, to ask how Minnesota might obtain federal approval to experiment. Ford's team dubbed itself the Cosmic Waiver Work Subgroup because it wanted a federal waiver big enough to cover every aspect of the social safety net.[2]

During that summer, however, Minnesota's path toward welfare reform would take an important turn. In other states, the cause attracted prominent political patrons. Governors Tommy Thompson in Wisconsin and John Engler in Michigan, and later Mayor Rudolph Giuliani in New York City, embraced specific antipoverty tactics, put political muscle behind the effort, and then boasted personally of the results. In Minnesota, no such star patron emerged. Governor Perpich encouraged his staff to experiment, but spent his time on a broader state agenda of education and economic development. Commissioner Sandra Gardebring embraced the concept of redesigning welfare and transmitted it to her staff, but she would be preoccupied for the next two years with more urgent crises in the state's nursing homes and state hospitals. Keith Ford, who had the closest personal relationship with Perpich, would himself be out of a job within two years when the legislature shuttered the Office of Jobs Policy.

As a result, the long task of actually designing a new welfare system fell to career professionals at the state Department of Human Services. Theirs was the agency that oversaw AFDC, food stamps, and Medicaid in Minnesota, and sooner or later they would be the ones writing the rules and issuing the checks for any new public-assistance system. This meant a group of devoted but anonymous government employees would have to sell the concept intermittently to new political leaders. But it also meant they could design a system based on the best empirical research and field testing, not on some political slogan or ideological gimmick.

The design task fell chiefly to Joel Kvamme, whose methodical research had guided the welfare-reform commission and seemed to lie at the core of the state's new welfare-to-work philosophy. The political chores fell to Ford, a skilled lobbyist who worried about Perpich's legacy in a state where many families still were struggling economically. Bridging the technical and political tracks was an old friend and colleague of Kvamme's named John Petraborg. Petraborg had started at the Department of Human Services some years earlier as an aide to Kvamme in the area of county compliance and quality control. But he had a deft management style and a gift for distilling complicated ideas into compelling precepts. In 1987 Gardebring made him assistant commissioner for family support—the agency's top welfare official —a platform that would before long make him the key advocate for a new antipoverty strategy.

By late 1987 Kvamme had put together a small team of technicians to begin designing a new welfare-to-work apparatus. His first hire was Myra Segal, who had helped staff the welfare-reform commission and had just graduated from the University of Minnesota's Humphrey School of Public Affairs. Before long he hired another Humphrey Institute graduate, Nancy Vivian, and asked her to start looking into employment and training strategies. Chuck Johnson, though still on Ford's staff, began spending more time with the Human Services cadre, and Steve Rhodes pitched in with research and memos. Later the technical team would expand to include Joan Truhler, an expert in vocational training and client case management; JoAnn Lindstrom, a welfare supervisor from

Pine County who would write regulations manuals for county welfare workers; and Sheryl Lockwood, who had worked on the Human Services MAXIS computer system and understood how the computer would have to be reprogrammed to track new clients with new benefits and eligibility rules.

Kvamme's team started with four principles laid down by the welfare-reform commission, reasoning that the commission had articulated a set of consensus values widely held by Minnesotans. First was that welfare reform should lead to higher incomes for poor families. Kvamme's research showed that, because the legislature had failed to adjust AFDC benefits for inflation in many years, Minnesota's effective welfare grant had dropped by some 30 percent since the early 1970s. By the mid-1980s most families on assistance were living far below the federal poverty line[3] (although sociologists would later confirm what many people suspected, that many welfare recipients supplemented their benefit checks with off-the-books endeavors, including prostitution, domestic work, and baby-sitting). Yet work would not automatically lift them out of poverty: the 1980s had produced falling wages for most American workers and a surge in the number of working poor. A second principle was that Minnesota should try to preempt long-term welfare use. Kvamme's studies found a sharp increase in the number of welfare recipients who had never married and had borne babies out of wedlock. It also showed that these recipients were most likely to become long-term dependents.[4] A third principle was that any new system should expect and reward work from most recipients. As the Boxleitner-Johnson commission discovered, work had become the norm for American mothers in the 1970s and 1980s, and in memos to Perpich's cabinet Kvamme now asked whether the public would support a system in which welfare mothers were the exceptions who got to stay home.[5]

The fourth principle was simplification. Their days in AFDC quality control had convinced Kvamme and Petraborg that most cases of welfare "fraud" actually arose from errors made by county caseworkers trying to interpret or obey confusing regulations. Indeed, Kvamme would spend hours with his staff musing about "operational clarity" and "bringing cosmos to chaos," and they sometimes found it hard to tell which was his greater passion, creating better opportunities for poor families or simplifying a government bureaucracy whose clutter and intrusiveness seemed to offend him. But the goal was clear: if Minnesota could cut the paperwork and streamline the rules, it would reduce the amount of error in the system and, not coincidentally, increase the amount of time that county welfare workers could spend actually helping clients. Last, testimony to the welfare-reform commission had revealed that many families found the system overbearing and paternalistic. Kvamme and Petraborg argued that most welfare recipients were capable of acting responsibly, but only if the government gave them the opportunity.

Although these principles seemed attractive and even intuitive, they had long ago disappeared into the murk of accumulated federal regulations, and reviving them would require Kvamme's team to solve several vexing design problems.

The first of these was what Myra Segal called "the slope." To reward employment, Minnesota had to show welfare recipients that their income would actually rise as they made the transition from welfare to work. That wasn't the case under AFDC in the 1980s. Federal rules said that when state authorities calculated a recipient's welfare benefit, they had to count any earned income and then reduce her grant almost a dollar for each dollar of earnings. In other words, the recipient's income slope was essentially horizontal if she went to work. But there was a tool, known in the parlance as an "earnings disregard," which allowed the state to ignore part of a recipient's earnings in the grant calculation, allowing her to keep her paycheck and part of her welfare grant. A recipient who received $500 per month in welfare, then took a job paying $500 per month, would be able to keep her earnings and a portion of her welfare check, for a total monthly income of perhaps $750 per month, depending on the amount of the earnings disregard. Earnings disregards had been in and out of the AFDC rule book several times, but economists were skeptical about their effectiveness in the early 1980s and the technique had been sharply curtailed in the early years of the Reagan administration. Kvamme's research, however, showed that the number of working welfare families in Minnesota fell sharply after the earnings disregard disappeared. Finding a way to restore it seemed like a natural first step if Minnesota wanted to reward work and reduce poverty.

Yet specifying the size of the disregard was tricky. If it were too small, recipients might ignore the incentive. Why would a struggling single mother take the trouble of hunting for work, arranging child care, buying a new wardrobe, and putting up with a harried work schedule for an extra $10 or $20 a week of income? On the other hand, if the disregard were too generous, it would let recipients stay on welfare long after they began to earn sizable paychecks and, in effect, load up the welfare rolls with working families. Worse, it would risk a problem known as "opt in": the temptation of working families to apply for welfare just to get an earnings supplement. In the end, after poring over econometric studies of income incentives and their behavioral effects, Kvamme's team settled on two devices to raise the income slope. First, any welfare recipient who found work would automatically receive a higher monthly benefit, a grant known as the family wage level, 20 percent larger than the basic welfare grant. That would give recipients an instant reward for finding work. Second, they proposed an income disregard of 38 percent, so that a recipient could continue moving up the income scale without constant financial penalties. Combining the two devices meant that a recipient would receive an instant reward for going to work and could bring home more and more income as she worked more hours or earned higher wages, until she finally worked her way off assistance at 140 percent of the federal poverty level.

A second design puzzle required the state to decide which clients would receive intensive help from their county welfare offices. Governors in some states were insisting on "universal engagement," a mandate that counties place every welfare recipient in a job or job training immediately. But that sort of supervision was labor intensive and costly; it might require counties to double or triple their welfare staffs. Here Kvamme's instincts were rather conservative, and once again his research suggested a solution. His longitudinal studies showed that most welfare recipients got off assistance within a year or two pretty much by themselves and without much help from the county. Why require costly and intrusive case management from day one for clients who could rather quickly find work on their own? Kvamme's group wound up recommending that new welfare applicants be given two years to put their lives together while collecting a benefit check; only at that point would a caseworker step in and offer intensive supervision.[6] But Kvamme's research also had raised worries about recipients who stayed on assistance for more than two years; a system that neglected them ran a high risk of creating long-term welfare users. In a departure from PATHS, the new system said that any recipient who had been on assistance for two out of the previous three years would have to find work, at a minimum of thirty hours per week, or come into a county welfare office for mandatory employment services and job counseling.

Even as Kvamme's team put their trust in the labor market, however, most of their colleagues in the department believed that

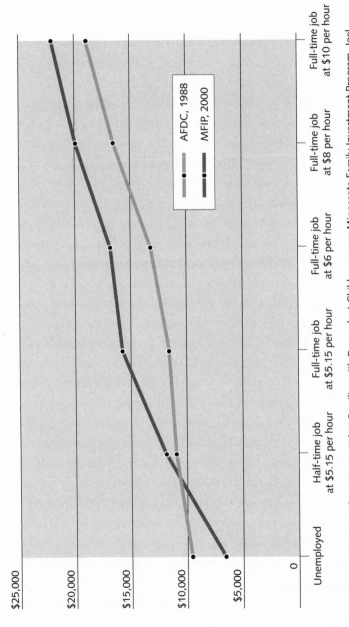

Total annual income of recipients, Aid to Families with Dependent Children versus Minnesota Family Investment Program. Joel Kvamme's team changed the welfare-benefit structure to reward employment: the income slope of an MFIP recipient who found work would rise much more rapidly than the income slope of a recipient in the former system, AFDC.

some welfare families would never become self-sufficient through work. AFDC had over the years become a catchall system that supported not only the victims of layoffs and divorces, but also adults with mental illness, parents of disabled children, victims of severe domestic violence, and troubled adults with other chronic problems. So Kvamme and Segal began drafting a series of "good cause" exemptions to the system's work requirements: lack of adequate child care, illness of a family member that required full-time attention, and chronic disability or work-related injury.[7]

Though the new system would be built substantially on trust and rewards, the group also realized that it would need an enforcement mechanism. Compared with the PATHS program, it would place bigger demands on welfare recipients and push them toward the job market more quickly. Kvamme's colleagues argued it would need enforcement tools for recipients who resisted the new work message. In early 1988 Segal and Vivian conducted a series of focus groups with welfare recipients and local caseworkers, and they heard plenty about families who gamed the system—working for cash and hiding it from the county, or living surreptitiously with boyfriends—or who simply resisted all attempts at motivation. So they built in a "sanction," a 10-percent benefit cut for any client who refused to comply with the self-sufficiency work requirements.

Kvamme's small design team continued this work for the better part of nine months, ordering data runs from department statisticians, testing their ideas with focus groups, consulting Petraborg, Gardebring, and Keith Ford.

By the summer of 1988 the Cosmic Waiver Work Subgroup had the outlines of a revamped welfare system, and on August 4 Governor Perpich unveiled it for reporters. He would combine several assistance programs, including AFDC and food stamps, to simplify the welfare application process and consolidate it around a program that rewarded work. He would restructure cash benefits so that the new system rewarded work. And he would create broad, new subsidies to help poor single parents pay for child care as they entered the job market. Because the strategy was so novel, the Department of Human Services would test it in a handful of counties and hire an independent national evaluator to measure its results. The strategy, which had gone under many names during its gestation period, would be called the Minnesota Family Investment Plan.

When the legislature convened in January 1989, Perpich and Gardebring asked a bipartisan pair of respected senators, Democrat John Brandl and Republican minority leader Duane Benson, to sponsor the bill. The house author would be Lee Greenfield, a veteran of the 1986 battle and a trusted legislative tactician. At the bill's first committee hearing, a welfare caseworker from Hennepin County unwound a sheaf of papers twenty-nine and a half feet long and explained that this was the amount of paperwork needed to enroll one client on public assistance in the existing system. Testifying for the administration's overhaul, Petraborg said, "We want to throw out that system and start from scratch."[8] That spring the MFIP bill passed both chambers by large margins and Perpich signed it into law.

Designing a better welfare system for Minnesota was one thing. Selling it to federal authorities would be quite another. Two years earlier, when Perpich had first encouraged his cabinet to experiment with family assistance, Gardebring and Petraborg had flown to Washington to sound out the Reagan administration on Minnesota's strategy. Their contact at the White House was Charles Hobbs, Reagan's chief adviser on state welfare innovation. The two got a cordial welcome in Hobbs's palatial office but a disappointing answer: welfare reform in the Reagan administration meant tightening rules and cutting caseloads, quite the opposite of the Minnesota philosophy.[9]

Somewhat daunted by that reception, Petraborg and his staff had consulted their counterparts in other states. They discovered that Washington State had secured permission for an experiment with food stamps and AFDC by circumventing the White House and going straight to Congress. With support from its own congressional delegation, a state could get a special law that would order the appropriate cabinet agencies—in this case the Department of Agriculture and the Department of Health and Human Services—to grant the necessary waivers.

In the summer of 1989 Minnesota embarked on the same track. But as Petraborg prepared for a summer of lobbying, he found that his task had changed markedly in the two years since his visit to Charles Hobbs. To get authorizing legislation through a Democratic Congress meant securing the support of key Democratic committee chairs, including Senator Patrick Leahy of the Agriculture Committee and Representative Dan Rostenkowski of Ways and Means. That, in turn, meant securing the approval of influential advocacy groups, such as the Children's Defense Fund and the Center on Budget and Policy Priorities. Many of these advocates, such as Robert Greenstein at the Center on Budget and Policy Priorities, had themselves played roles in the War on Poverty during the 1960s and 1970s, and then had spent the 1980s watching the Reagan administration dismantle the federal social safety net. They were skeptical when governors came calling with their own schemes to overhaul venerable federal social programs.

Week after week through the summer of 1989, Petraborg and a colleague, Julie Brunner, called on congressional committee staffers and the advocacy community, arguing that Minnesota planned to broaden the social safety net, not shred it. Analysts at the Children's Defense Fund or the Food Research and Action Center would review a draft of the plan, find flaws or omissions, and ask the Minnesota contingent to redraft it. Petraborg ran up

quickly discovered a lighthearted way to communicate the change. Since the New York evaluators wanted to compare MFIP's results with those of the old welfare system, they divided every new batch of welfare applicants by random assignment, with half going into AFDC and half going into MFIP's new array of services and benefits. As they marveled at the big wage supplements, expansive work supports, and employment services of MFIP, the Lifetrack staff would joke with clients assigned to MFIP, saying, "Congratulations. You've won the lottery."

CHAPTER 5

Real Life, Winter 2001–2002

Meg is sitting at her kitchen table, working on a household budget and feeling that perhaps her life is not disintegrating after all. There are two gallons of milk in the refrigerator, a big jar of applesauce for the baby, and a quart of lemon yogurt—the only nutritious food the boys will eat with any enthusiasm. The pantry is stocked with pasta, spaghetti sauce, and rice, and there's enough chicken in the freezer to make meals for a month.

It's mid-January and Meg has received her first check from Ramsey County. Actually, in the modern world of welfare, it's not a check but a debit card backed by a monthly deposit directly into her bank account. She has caught up on her rent and, for the first time since October, put a full tank of gas in her car. Tonight she is trying to figure out who to pay next. She's a month behind on her phone bill, now $62. With a steady schedule of doctor appointments for the children and job interviews for herself, she can't afford to have the line cut off. Or she could repay part of the $300 she borrowed from her brother in November. It's the first time in three months that she has felt the luxury of deploying money as she sees fit.

The county also has come through with medical coverage

and, for the first time in almost three years, Meg and her children all have the same health insurance. For a year after her divorce she patched together coverage from several sources. Medicaid, the federal-state health program for poor families, known in Minnesota as Medical Assistance, covered the children. But its eligibility threshold is higher for adults, and Meg didn't qualify. For a time she bought health insurance for herself through her hotel job, but soon she couldn't afford the $90 monthly premium. Then she turned to a third option, a state program called Minnesota-Care, designed for the working poor. MinnesotaCare requires that applicants be uninsured for four months before entering, so she had to take the risk and go without coverage, then come up with the money to cover a subsidized premium of $65 per month. By November, however, even that was beyond her means.

Having an insurance card in her billfold is a great relief, since Zachary gets frequent ear infections and Samuel is due for a checkup with the pediatrician. But Medicaid has come to resemble any other type of health insurance in the managed-care era: it simply enrolled Meg in a local HMO and left her to fend for the best care possible. Like any other parent, she has learned that you have to fight for good health care and, after four phone calls and much negotiation, she got her favorite clinic at Children's Hospital of St. Paul to accept Medicaid. The clinic has a pediatrician Meg trusts, and it's a short drive when she has to bundle up all three children for a doctor's appointment on short notice.

These crises settled, she is able to contemplate her household finances. Until she finds work, she will collect a monthly benefit of $981, which includes a cash grant of $621 and $360 from the food-stamp program. With that she can safely cover her rent, $520 per month, buy groceries, pay her utility bills, and still have another $20 a week to put gas in the car or make the occasional trip to Target.

Zachary bounds into the room and stands at the kitchen table, peering at his mother's calculations. Meg strokes his hair somewhat distractedly and asks what he wants for supper tomorrow night. Macaroni and cheese, he says, but only if he gets to do the cooking. He's growing up and beginning to show an independent streak. It doesn't take her long to run the scenario through her imagination. "Boiling water? Hot pans? I don't think so. How about if you try scrambled eggs?"

The boys don't know what welfare is, but they can detect a reduced level of tension around the apartment now that Meg has enough money to pay her bills. For the last three months they have heard a lot of "no's" from their mother—no lunch at McDonald's, no new Legos, no Saturday afternoons at the movies—and they quickly learned not to beg for treats when their mom got a certain grim look on her face. Meg has had more time for them since being unemployed—at least when the baby was sleeping—but they could hear a certain tightness and distraction in her voice.

Christmas, of course, was a disaster. She had raised them to believe that the holiday marked the birth of Jesus, not an occasion for Hot Wheels and Gobots. Even so, she knew that little boys expect toys under the Christmas tree. "I told them that sometimes it's better not to get something new. Because when you get new things you don't appreciate what you already had."

Now their mother seems more at ease, and there is even money in the household budget for a few minor luxuries—a box of Cocoa Puffs in the pantry and a Disney video on Friday night.

Having finished with her checkbook, Meg turns to a stack of MFIP work sheets from the overview class at Lifetrack Resources. She found the class itself rather rudimentary, even patronizing. A frown of concentration comes over her face and she sighs with the impatience that comes over her when the rest of the world isn't moving as fast as she thinks it should. "It was for people who haven't worked before. I'd already done all the things they said. I knew about the child-care assistance, I had made my list of goals."

But the work sheets prove more useful. If she finds a job, she will immediately qualify for a higher benefit from the county—$1,079 per month, up from the $981 she receives now as a single parent with three children. The new grant will be reduced as she starts earning more money, but not eliminated. As a result, she sees that, just as the program promised, her take-home income will climb steadily as she works more hours. If she works half-time at $8 per hour, she will take home $1,340 each month, counting her earnings and a partial MFIP grant. If she gets a full-time job at $10 per hour, her monthly earnings would rise to almost $1,740 and she would leave cash assistance.

This is the arithmetic that her job counselor emphasized at their first meeting. He pointed out that if she could get a full-time job at just $7 she would have enough income, combining her earnings and a partial MFIP grant, to take home more than $18,000 a year and lift her family above the poverty line. This would also qualify her for the federal Earned Income Tax Credit and a similar state tax credit, programs that give direct cash refunds to low-wage workers, which could give her an additional $3,000 at the end of the year.

In the booming job market of the late 1990s, that's the advice that many job counselors were giving their Minnesota Family Investment Program clients. Research showed that employers were skeptical of job applicants who had dropped out of the job market for long spells, and so state and county job counselors encouraged MFIP clients to get jobs as fast as possible. Veteran caseworkers also remembered welfare mothers from earlier welfare-reform projects who had enrolled in local community colleges without clear career goals, subsisted for months on welfare and no paycheck, and then never successfully made the transition from school to work. They were inclined to recommend work, or a combination of school and work, to all but the most talented and determined clients. Finally, MFIP job counselors were mindful of the federal five-year cap on cash benefits. If Meg could get a job at $10 per hour, she could go off the cash portion of her county grant, keep her food-stamp benefit, and stop her federal clock from ticking. That would keep months of coverage in the bank for emergencies in the future.

Many MFIP clients accepted this advice readily. They had never felt successful in school in the first place, and they were eager to bring home a paycheck again. But the job counselor's advice only brings out the independent streak in Meg. "He just wants me to get a job. He said there must be gas stations in my neighborhood that need cashiers!" She knows that $7 an hour will never provide her children the kind of life she wants for them, and that a job behind a cash register is unlikely to lead to anything better. She also knows that skilled clerical workers can earn $12 an hour or more and qualify for a decent package of fringe benefits. She's even looked into a St. Paul vocational school that offers certification in Microsoft Office software, and she knows that holding that diploma would improve her earnings prospects hugely.

Before her job counselor will approve vocational school, however, Meg must complete a state questionnaire called an Occupational Research Packet. It's a daunting six-page document that requires Meg to research the number of job openings and pay rates in her desired occupation and even to interview potential employers to see if they actually hire graduates of the school in question. Job counselors had found the packet, with its demanding requirements, to be a good predictor of whether a client will actually succeed in school. To Meg, it's one more needless barrier. "Why can't they just say yes?" she asks, her voice squeaking with frustration.

In this tug of war with her job counselor, Meg reveals a broader struggle within MFIP and within the national welfare-to-work debate. The 1996 federal welfare law put enormous pressure on states and counties to move welfare recipients directly into work. A large body of research showed that elegant education and job-training programs of the past had produced only modest gains in the employment and earnings of poor adults, and that going to work quickly was often the best way for a welfare parent to raise her income and reduce her use of welfare. But there were nuances to this story. While it was true that pure education strategies often flopped, research also showed that pure work-first strategies produced little long-term progress for welfare clients. A handful of studies suggested that so-called "mixed strategies"—those that encouraged clients to choose their first jobs carefully, then combine work with work-specific training—produced the biggest income gains over a period of a few years.[1] While many welfare clients plainly lacked the motivation and experience to take advantage of higher education, it seemed perfect for ambitious clients like Meg.

Meanwhile, Meg is also thinking about taking a Spanish class. Scanning the Help Wanted ads, she noticed that many employers want bilingual employees. "Anything that makes me more marketable," she says, stuffing the paperwork back in a folder. "You are not going to tell me no," she says resolutely. "Either way I go, I'm going to get somewhere."

Patty has no quarrel with the work-first philosophy of MFIP. When I catch up with her again, on a late afternoon in mid-January, she's dressing for work and waiting for the baby-sitter. She's been on assistance for less than two months and already has found a job at a nearby nightspot called the Blainebrook Bowl. "I'm not crazy about bartending," she says. "But it's nice to know that *somebody* wants you. And, hey, it's ready cash."

Patty brings a pragmatic, almost mercenary, attitude to most projects in her life, and she has wasted no time in figuring out how MFIP will work for her. She went home from the orientation class at Anoka County, studied the various handouts, and quickly realized that her monthly grant would increase the minute she found work—from $651 to $716 for a household of two—and that she would have more money in her pocket almost instantly. The child-care subsidy isn't a big draw for her; Samantha goes to bed shortly after Patty leaves for work in the evening and Patty reckons that her new boyfriend, Don, can watch the girl along with his own two sons if need be. But another benefit has caught her eye: if she works thirty hours a week for a thirty-day stretch, she will qualify for an interest-free $2,300 car loan through a program sponsored by the McKnight Foundation, a big Minneapolis philanthropy with an interest in welfare reform. Since Ethyl the truck died, Patty has been driving Don's second car, a used Chevy Camaro. It's a muscle car that appeals to the rebel in her, and he seems in no hurry to get it back. But she would be happier if she owned it outright. "I'll scan groceries if that's what it takes to get thirty hours a week," she says. "That car loan is exactly what I need."

Patty also thinks that work sets an important example for Samantha. She is not poetic about the nobility of labor; she just thinks that Samantha will learn some important practical lessons from seeing her mother go off to work. "She's got to understand where money comes from," Patty says. "Anything that she gets, it's going to come from me, because her dad sure doesn't have the money to buy her anything."

At a deeper level, Patty is eager to work because she has never quite made peace with accepting welfare. She prides herself on a rebellious streak, but she also thinks of herself as a daughter of the respectable suburban middle class, and as someone who has fended for herself for years and paid her share of taxes. "I never pictured myself in a welfare office," she told me the first time we spoke.

For exactly this reason, Patty likes the Anoka County system. She was a bit overwhelmed by the first day's orientation session. "God, I was still unpacking that morning. I couldn't even find clean underwear, and I had to show up for five hours of class!" But everything else about the county system appeals to her. In Anoka County, MFIP recipients use the same workforce center as anyone else—be they laid-off factory workers or new college graduates—which reduces the sense of stigma she might other-wise feel. And her job counselor treats her as an adult as long as she calls in once a month and reports that she is either working or looking for work. "I don't like anybody judging me, you know? But these people are professionals. They don't care what your story is. Their job is to get you back on your feet."

Better yet, her financial worker says the county will help her enforce a child-support order from Samantha's father. Patty estimates that she's received less than $2,500 from him in the seven years since she walked out, or less than $30 a month. Until now, Patty has felt that she got nothing but the runaround from government authorities. "Hennepin County said, no, your court order was entered in Wright County. Go there. In Wright County they said, no, you don't live here anymore. Go to the county where you live.

"But what's the point? The child-support order was $58 per month. Are you kidding? I pay more for school lunches!"

In Anoka County, if she cooperates with the work require-ments and the child-support paperwork, they might help her collect more money without protracted legal skirmishing.

Though Patty describes the episode with a cynical laugh, the lack of child-support payments from absent fathers is one of the most serious and bedeviling problems in welfare reform. Since the great majority of adult welfare recipients are single mothers, welfare reform is, at some level, about fathers who cannot or will not support their children. Scholars estimate that only half to two-thirds of poor and middle-income single mothers receive any child support from noncustodial fathers, and well less than half receive the full amount owed to them.[2] In fiscal year 2000, it appeared that mothers and governments collected only $13 billion out of $23 billion in current child-support obligations and only $6 billion out of $84 billion in arrearages.[3]

One problem is that many of the noncustodial fathers are as broke and disorganized as the mothers. Two hundred dollars a month would only begin to pay the costs of raising a child today, but it's an overwhelming sum to fathers who work at low wages and have frequent bouts of unemployment. A second problem is that poor mothers tend to move frequently, which means that different counties and different states have to cooperate in tracking down mothers and fathers and delivering child-support payments. Still, scholars estimate that child support, where paid, lifts 5 to 7 percent of eligible parents out of poverty[4] and it reduced welfare caseloads by 12 to 17 percent in the middle 1990s.[5]

Improved child-support enforcement is also one of the obscure but significant successes of welfare policy in the late 1990s. Congress passed a series of child-support enforcement laws in 1984, 1988, and 1996, with the result that the share of welfare mothers who received child-support payments nearly doubled, from 13 percent to 25 percent, between 1978 and 1998.[6]

In Patty's case, the picture will be a little more complicated. Many states, including Minnesota, historically withheld any child-support payments they collected on behalf of welfare parents as a means of recouping government spending on welfare. In 2001, Minnesota began passing along these child-support payments from the absent parent to the custodial parent, but it also reduced the custodial parent's MFIP grant accordingly.

Patty finds this confusing and annoying. "I thought child-support was supposed to help me out. Instead, they're going to dock my grant."

If Patty can work her way off MFIP, however, she would get to keep any child-support payments she collected from Mike. And that monthly sum could make a big difference in paying Samantha's bills and keeping Patty off welfare in the future.

The question of child support raises another point that grates on Patty: the furor over welfare invariably demonizes single mothers more than the fathers of their children. Almost 90 percent of welfare adults are single parents, and probably 80 percent are single mothers. By cracking down on welfare usage, Congress has in effect cracked down on single mothers. And despite the various reforms in child-support collection, the fathers of their children are often an afterthought in the blame game. Patty doesn't pay much attention to debates in Congress or social science, but she knows plenty about irresponsible fathers.

"I've got three girlfriends who are divorced. Every one of them, when they send their kids off for a weekend with their dads, they have to make up a care package—bread, mac and cheese, fruit. Otherwise, they know their kids won't eat right.

"Samantha went off ice-fishing with her father last winter. All they ate for a weekend was fish and scrambled eggs! Last weekend he was going to take her again. He begged me to pack up some groceries before he came and got her. He said he didn't have anything in the house. I said, 'Go to a food shelf! That's what I'm going to have to do!' So I packed up some noodles—she loves mac and cheese—and some juice. I sent a whole can of juice! That would have lasted me a week."

Patty pauses for a moment and grows more reflective. However much she despises Samantha's father, she also blames herself for a series of foolish choices and misanthropic episodes over the years. For all her wild adolescence and party-girl swagger, Patty has been tamed a bit by raising a daughter, and she has had long hours to sit with her regrets and lost aspirations. She makes time every day, in the afternoon or at bedtime, to read to Samantha. Their current book is *Charlotte's Web*, which was Patty's own childhood favorite. It's a curiously sentimental choice for someone so tough-minded as Patty. But as a girl she spent summers on an uncle's farm in Iowa, and there is something about E. B. White's community of animals, loyal to each other and protective against the predations of humans, that appealed to her for years. And then there was Charlotte, the unlikely heroine, the ugly outsider who, through an act of unlooked-for sacrifice, actually managed to achieve something noble. "I read it over and over again," Patty says. "I want her to love it too. I want her to read it on her own when she starts reading. I want her to do better than I did."

On a Tuesday morning in the Osseo Area Public Schools' Adult Basic Ed program, Libby Ames is prepping her students for their high-school equivalency exams in English composition. Her classroom is a remodeled dentist's office in a suburban strip mall two blocks from Lucille's apartment. The class, fourteen adults clustered around a rectangular table in the cramped room, consists of five African Americans, three Hispanic Americans, two Hmong immigrants, and four West African refugees.

"OK," Ames begins. "This exam asks you to write an essay stating your opinion on whether fast food is good or bad. Opinion means that you get to give your point of view, so I want you to start by writing down some reasons why you think fast food is good."

After a few minutes she starts calling on her students. "Frances?"

"Fast food is good because you don't have to cook. It saves you time."

"Great. William?"

"Fast food is good because you can get it any time, like late at night on your way home from work."

"Good. Nick?"

"It's cheap. And sometimes it's delicious."

"Wow. That's one I hadn't heard before. OK, now you have several reasons why you could make an argument that fast food is good. You're set up and you can start writing your essay. How do you like to get started writing? Rose?"

"I take about three sheets of paper. I write it out once. Then I start over and write it again. Then I write my final draft."

"That's a good technique. But why might it not work when you're taking the GED?"

A long pause. "Because it takes too long," William observes.

"Exactly. When you're taking a timed test, you won't have time to write your rough draft and a final draft. So when you're taking the test, make sure you've got your ideas, then take the time to brainstorm a little and organize your thoughts before you actually start writing."

"OK, we meet again on Thursday. Bring in your work so I can see how far you've gotten. Good luck with your brainstorming."

Libby Ames's classroom in Adult Basic Ed is where Lucille landed in the fall of 2001, after she reapplied for welfare, was assigned to an employment-services agency called Hired, and drew Patty Czech as her job counselor. Czech took one look at

Lucille's track record in the workplace and decided that sending her back into the low-wage job market was pointless. A standardized abilities test showed Lucille to have an IQ of seventy. That can qualify as a vocational disability under federal law, and it meant that Lucille was probably unprepared for most of the clerical and health-care jobs to which Czech referred many clients. But Lucille also had a chronic back ailment. A doctor had put her on painkillers and certified that she could not stand for long periods, which meant that she probably could not hold the sort of lucrative light-assembly jobs that seemed to work well for many suburban MFIP clients. Moreover, Lucille seemed genuinely regretful about having dropped out of high school as a teenager and genuinely eager to take another crack at the books. And so Czech referred her to Adult Basic Education in her local school district, Osseo Area Schools, District 279.

On a first visit, the Adult Basic Ed program is not inspiring. It's housed in a squat professional building on a suburban stretch of Zane Avenue in Brooklyn Park. It shares a parking lot with a strip mall that houses a liquor store, a convenience store, two barbershops, a CD shop, and a diner. The tiny parking lot is crammed with rusting Toyota and Ford sedans and busy with mothers pushing babies in strollers. It was originally home to a cluster of dental clinics, and even today the interior is chopped up into cubbyhole offices. When Lucille arrives one morning, the tiny lunchroom is packed with Somali women gossiping playfully and making coffee. In the computer lab, four Hmong students sit at computer screens working on vocabulary. Down the hall, an instructor is drilling an advanced English class on the use of past-tense constructions.

But Lucille is comfortable here. Her apartment at Huntington Place is just a five-minute walk away, which is crucial because, even at age thirty-one, she doesn't have a driver's license. And because Adult Basic Ed has its own building, Lucille isn't thrown in with a bunch of teenagers. Most of the other students are quite like her, either immigrants with little formal education or MFIP clients who dropped out of school before mastering basic grammar and arithmetic.

If Adult Basic Ed makes a good fit for Lucille, it also shows the flexibility of MFIP. The Personal Responsibility Act encouraged states to push work rather than schooling, and it was only because Minnesota already had a waiver from federal welfare regulations that it could still offer MFIP recipients a broad range of schooling choices as alternatives to work.

Even so, as Meg had discovered, MFIP job counselors didn't approve schooling for every client. In Hennepin County, where Lucille lives, employment-service vendors had to meet strict performance targets, such as placing a certain share of clients in jobs and moving clients off assistance. Each client placed in school could dilute the agency's performance against county goals. Then, too, the vendors had limited budgets for tuition and other school-related costs. There was also some risk for Lucille. She had been on and off public assistance several times during the 1990s, with the result that she already had used up many months of her federal cash benefits. If she stayed on MFIP now, she was scheduled to exhaust her cash benefits in the fall of 2003, and she couldn't afford to spend endless months in a classroom. Nonetheless, Patty Czech thought school was worth a try. It seemed plain to her that Lucille had made several good-faith efforts to find work in the past, and that these were doomed to fail until she improved her basic reading and writing skills. Then, too, Adult Basic Education would be a sort of test. If Lucille thrived and earned her degree, she would have a better shot at getting work. If she foundered, then Hired would have a little extra information about her cognitive abilities and her prospects for independent employment.

Lucille is direct and unabashed about her intellectual limits. Describing her attempt to train for a driver's license, she says, "My cousin took me out for some driving lessons. But I didn't do so well and she lost patience pretty quick." Of her efforts in the classroom she says, "I'm pretty good at math. I passed my test on that right away. But language—I don't know. That's hard for me. It has always given me trouble."

In December, however, Lucille scored a triumph. After three months in Adult Basic Ed she passed her final exams and graduated from Class Four to Class Five. This would be the last step before entering the GED program, the top rung in the program and a source of evident desire for Lucille. "I have a friend who works at Hennepin County," she says. "She says that if I can get my GED and pass typing, I can get a good county job."

CHAPTER 6

A New Federal Challenge (1997):
The Personal Responsibility Act
Threatens Minnesota's Innovations

On January 21, 1997, Governor Arne Carlson invited reporters to his office at the state capitol for an update on Minnesota's welfare-to-work project. Results were trickling in from the county field trials and Minnesota had some boasting to do. Evaluators from the Manpower Demonstration Research Corporation had found that, in most counties, the Minnesota Family Investment Program increased employment among long-term welfare recipients, increased their overall household incomes, and reduced the number of families living in poverty.[1] The results covered only the early months of MFIP's startup and the evaluators warned that they were provisional, but Carlson embraced them proudly.

Carlson's news conference, three years into the MFIP field trials, signaled that MFIP had passed two critical tests. First, it could deliver the results its designers intended. The seven test counties had remodeled their welfare offices and introduced thousands of poor families to a simple system with a powerful pro-work message. By recasting welfare's incentives and creating tangible rewards for work, the new approach could promote self-reliance among welfare families while also helping them to escape poverty.

Second, MFIP had survived a tricky political transition from the Democratic governor who sired it to his Republican successor. After defeating Rudy Perpich in 1990, Arne Carlson had announced a new era of fiscal austerity and jettisoned much of his predecessor's imaginative agenda. But Carlson was a social moderate, even a dove, on children's issues. Despite his Swedish surname and midwestern affect, he had grown up poor in a rough neighborhood of New York City. He liked balanced budgets, but he was no welfare-basher. So when John Petraborg, now the acting commissioner of Minnesota's Department of Human Services, approached Carlson periodically for funds to continue the MFIP field trials, he had little trouble selling the new Republican governor on a program that promoted work while reducing poverty.

Now, however, MFIP faced a new and bigger challenge. While Minnesota had been pursuing its quiet little experiment in family incentives, welfare reform had emerged as a front-burner controversy in Washington, D.C. President Bill Clinton had come to office in 1993 promising to "end welfare as we know it" and speaking earnestly of a time-limited system with strong work supports. But when he let the issue languish for two years, his Republican rivals in the House of Representatives seized it for their own. The Republican welfare bill, first introduced in 1995, was much tougher than the overhaul Clinton had planned. It not only required work of most welfare recipients, it also placed a five-year lifetime limit on cash benefits for most families. But it had little of the job-training money Clinton had planned and none of the funds for public jobs of last resort. It ordered states to move huge numbers of welfare recipients into the labor force, and it kicked hundreds of thousands of legal immigrants off various forms of public aid. Clinton vetoed the bill twice. But in the summer of 1996 Republicans passed the bill for a third time and Clinton, who feared losing centrist voters in the November presidential election, signed it on August 22, 1996.

By abolishing AFDC and by placing time limits on cash assistance, the Personal Responsibility and Work Opportunity Reconciliation Act brought the most sweeping changes to anti-poverty policy in sixty years. The political impact in Washington was seismic. Three of Clinton's most influential advisers at the Department of Health and Human Services—Peter Edelman, Wendell Primus, and Mary Jo Bane—resigned in protest. Social conservatives were euphoric: they felt that Washington had for the first time since the New Deal adopted a welfare system that expected work of almost all recipients and imposed meaningful penalties.

But it was the law's third major provision that caught the attention of the nation's governors and Petraborg's team at Human Services. The law abolished the old federal regulations on cash assistance and said that states were free, within certain new federal guidelines, to invent their own welfare systems. As long as it met federal employment targets, a state could decide when welfare recipients must work, how they might be rewarded, and how they would be punished for failure to comply. In short, it was the sweeping waiver that Minnesota had labored so strenuously to achieve seven years earlier. Only now states had to design and adopt their new welfare systems within twelve months.

Within a few weeks Carlson decided that MFIP would be Minnesota's blueprint for this new assistance system. Its creators now held influential positions in the administration: John Petraborg was acting commissioner of Human Services, Joel Kvamme was supervising the county field tests, and Deborah Huskins, the assistant attorney general who had helped draft the federal waivers in 1989, was now at Human Services as an assistant commissioner. While many states would have to start from scratch under the new federal directives, Minnesota already had a system backed by careful research and painstaking design. County welfare directors liked its simplicity; local field tests were beginning to work out the operational bugs. Best of all, welfare families seemed to be responding to its incentives.

Even so, taking MFIP statewide presented a new set of political and technical challenges. The little pilot project would have to meet the demanding and intricate requirements of the new federal law, especially time limits and work-participation targets. It would also have to win the support of elected officials and professional staff in the dozens of counties that had never participated in the field tests.

In the fall of 1996, Petraborg and Huskins asked Kevin Kelleher, a county commissioner from southeastern Minnesota and president of the Association of Minnesota Counties, to convene a task force of county officials. The group also included Susan Haigh, a county commissioner from Ramsey County and later chair of the Ramsey County board, and representatives from other rural and suburban counties. This group hashed out broad policy questions: Would counties accept the antipoverty thrust of MFIP? What tools would counties need to meet the big logistical challenges such as transportation in rural areas and immigrant services in urban zones? The county commissioners also feared that the legislature would impose ambitious work targets without sufficient funds for job training, child care, transportation, and other work supports, and they prepared to make their case at the state capitol. For more technical matters, Huskins and her staff consulted the Minnesota Association of County Social Service Administrators, a group of county professionals who met monthly in St. Paul. This group advised the department on logistical issues such as computer programming and improving coordination between job counselors and child-care providers.

In addition to consulting county authorities, Huskins's staff occasionally invited advocates from groups such as the Children's Defense Fund and Legal Aid to department working groups at 444 Lafayette Road. This triggered some misgivings in the department, but Petraborg and Huskins argued that they were likely to learn from the advocates while averting protest and lawsuits later as legislation began moving at the legislature.

By this point, Minnesota's large poverty advocacy community was divided into two camps. One group, the Welfare Rights Committee, consisted mainly of current and former welfare recipients, and had emerged from the militant welfare-rights movement of the 1970s. Its members never accepted the premises of the federal law and later held raucous protests at the state capitol against precepts such as work requirements and time limits. A second camp consisted of lobbyists and professional advocates from the nonprofit and religious communities. They recognized that Minnesota would have to comply with the broad precepts of the federal law, but they wanted to be at the table when officials from the Carlson administration made decisions that could preserve or dilute MFIP. Many of these advocates were uneasy about the imperatives of the federal law and feared that state budget constraints would subvert the best elements of MFIP. But some of the advocates, such as Shawn Fremstad of the Legal Services Advocacy Project and Tarryl Clark of the Children's Defense Fund, had become expert in the nuances of the federal law and showed Huskins's staff how Minnesota might honor Congress's intent while maintaining the strengths of MFIP.

This consultation process was time-consuming and often fractious, but it proved valuable later, when Human Services staff had to advise legislators on crucial design questions. Ann Sessoms, a division director who worked for Huskins, recalled a meeting at the capitol some months later when legislators had to decide how much time counties should have to convert thousands of families from the old AFDC system to the new rules of MFIP. Lawmakers wanted counties to move fast, but Sessoms recalled the sorts of logistical problems that local staff had explained to Human Services weeks earlier. After struggling to explain these practical issues, Sessoms finally stood before the legislators and offered a metaphor: Imagine that you are remodeling the only bathroom in your house. You have to replace the plumbing, rewire the electricity, repaint the walls, and tile the floor, all without ever losing use of the toilet. Legislators granted the counties the ninety days they wanted.

Beyond these design questions, Petraborg and Huskins faced a larger and more daunting political question that went to the heart of Minnesota's antipoverty philosophy. Many other states had begun welfare experiments of their own in the months before the Personal Responsibility and Work Opportunity Reconciliation Act (PRWORA) became law, and most of them were moving in quite the opposite direction from Minnesota. Florida, an early innovator with its Family Transition Program, had just adopted tough work mandates, a four-year limit on welfare benefits, and a 100-percent sanction for families who defied the rules. Florida legislators indulged in no niceties about reducing poverty; they said that work was ennobling for welfare recipients whether or not it made them better off.[2] Michigan had adopted a welfare-to-work system that, though it paid generous cash benefits, imposed tough noncompliance penalties and wouldn't even let families apply for assistance until they had attended employment workshops.[3] Connecticut, another state with high cash benefits, imposed a twenty-one-month time limit on assistance to families with employable adults and adopted a 100-percent sanction for a family's third violation of the rules.[4] Even a liberal state like Massachusetts, which paid generous cash benefits and exempted nearly half its caseload from work requirements, had tacked to the right; it cut benefits to nonworking families by 2.75 percent to encourage employment, imposed a time limit of two years in any five-year period, and said that any welfare recipient who had a baby while on assistance would get no increase in her grant.[5]

These states were not exceptions. When the U.S. Department of Health and Human Services surveyed the various state welfare experiments under way by 1996, it found that twenty states had tightened AFDC's work requirements; thirty-two had enacted time limits of five years or less; twenty-three had adopted "full family sanctions," or the power to kick families off assistance entirely for failing to comply with work requirements; and nineteen had imposed "family caps," which denied any increase in benefits to a mother who had a baby while on public assistance.[6]

Of course, the nation's most celebrated welfare experiment was taking place right next door in Wisconsin, and it too looked much tougher than Minnesota's. Wisconsin had been experimenting with new welfare tactics since the late 1980s, mostly in small county pilot projects, and it moved quickly after passage of the new federal law, enacting a statewide welfare-to-work program known as Wisconsin Works, or W-2. To lawmakers in Minnesota, the Wisconsin strategy had several attractive features. It offered the nation's most generous child-care subsidies for poor families who found jobs. Its BadgerCare program, like MinnesotaCare, offered subsidized health insurance to a large population of the working poor. In addition, Wisconsin took a step that few states dared: it promised jobs, at public expense, to welfare recipients who could not find work in private industry. But W-2 also had several features that seemed punitive to Kvamme and Petraborg and to many Minnesota legislators. For example, rather than bringing AFDC recipients into a county office and converting them to the new welfare system, it simply cancelled their benefits and forced them to reapply for aid, often through a local job counselor who had been instructed to discourage new applications.[7] Though no one measured the impact of this "diversion" strategy, it was thought to have prevented thousands of needy families from re-entering the system. In addition, W-2 promised universal engagement, which meant that job counselors had to find a job or an activity for almost every client who applied for aid. This contradicted the simplicity principle of Joel Kvamme, who thought it faster and more efficient to let welfare applicants test the job market on their own for some months before getting employment services from the county. Wisconsin also required job counselors to decide quickly whether an applicant was employable. Applicants deemed employable were ineligible for cash benefits, even though later evaluations found that job counselors had to make these decisions too quickly and with scant information.[8] Even the provision of public jobs, or Community Service Jobs, seemed unwise to the Minnesotans. It was certainly compassionate to create work for the neediest applicants, but it also entailed the creation of a large, expensive, and intrusive public-works bureaucracy.

Minnesota had a long tradition of bucking national trends in social policy, and it could have ignored the coercive drift of Wisconsin and the other states. But the Personal Responsibility Act created grave risks for any state that strayed too far from the pack. By freeing states to write their own eligibility rules and work requirements, the law greatly increased the variation from one state to the next—and the incentive for poor families to move from strict states to permissive ones. Yet the law also offered cash rewards to states that cut their caseloads quickly, even if they did so by encouraging poor families to move to other, more hospitable states. Any state that chose to be an outlier—spending more on poor families, adopting a patient attitude toward work, welcoming new indigents—could find itself in financial peril. And because federal welfare funds now came in a fixed annual block grant, any increase in local welfare costs would become a liability of state taxpayers.

The new landscape meant that Petraborg, who had sold MFIP to the legislature periodically when the department needed funds to continue the field trials, would now have to sell it in the most compelling and practical terms. Worse, he could no longer count on unstinting support from Democrats. Their key committee chair in the senate, Don Samuelson of Brainerd, was a fiscal conservative who supported tough work requirements. He also favored a residency requirement—that is, a rule denying Minnesota's generous benefits to migrants from other states.[9] The Democrats' welfare deal maker in the house, Representative Loren Jennings of Rush City, was a brusque, self-made businessman; he had grown up with modest means and he sympathized with poor families, but he liked time limits and the politics of self-reliance.[10] And though Democrats controlled the house, they held only a 70–64 majority, which meant they couldn't afford to lose even three members on a crucial piece of legislation. For their part, Republican legislators were mollified by the fact that MFIP had the endorsement of a governor from their own party. But they were quite prepared to put up a fight if this new welfare system seemed to coddle the poor or put Minnesota taxpayers at risk.

To make matters worse, the Carlson administration could not afford a prolonged legislative fight. The federal law offered cash bonuses to states that actually implemented new welfare systems by July 1997, which meant that a bill would have to clear the legislature by April or May. That was early for major legislation to pass both houses, but the Department of Human Services needed the $30 million federal bonus if it were going to make MFIP's budget add up.

That fall, Huskins proposed a strategy to Petraborg and Carlson. She recommended that the governor appoint an informal welfare task force, a bipartisan group of knowledgeable lawmakers who would hash out the major elements of a bill before formal debate at the capitol. They could study the toughest technical issues, settle the most controversial points in a setting removed from partisan fireworks, and then serve as advocates who would carry the legislation through committees quickly. Carlson liked the plan, for a similar strategy had helped push health-care reform through the legislature six years earlier, and he asked party leaders in both chambers to give him twelve names. But Carlson remained anxious about getting the delicate legislation through the legislature. Late that autumn he appointed a new commissioner of Human Services, passing over Petraborg and choosing an old friend and policy veteran named David Doth. Doth had served as budget director during Carlson's first term, but he had worked under both Democrats and Republicans, in the Finance and Human Services departments, and, crucially, he was known as a deft hand with legislators.

The welfare task force, or "Gang of Twelve," as it came to be known, was not uncontroversial. Journalists claimed that the panel was going to conduct public business behind closed doors, a violation of Minnesota's open-meeting law. The Welfare Rights Committee accused legislators of hiding their work from poor families, the very people who would be most affected. Doth finessed the issue: he didn't publicize the panel's meeting times and dates, but he didn't exclude anyone who showed up.

Despite its controversial provenance, the Gang of Twelve soon proved its value. Two times a week, after the legislature had finished its formal business for the day, the group would steal off down a tunnel from the capitol basement to the Centennial Office Building one block away and convene for four or five hours at a conference room of the State Planning Agency. The first meetings took the form of tutorials, with Doth or Huskins leading the legislators through provisions of the new federal law and explaining what it required of Minnesota. Soon they began working through the key design choices. Would Minnesota adopt the federal time limit, or something shorter, or something longer? Did legislators want to provide a safety net for immigrants who faced the loss of various federal benefits? Who might be exempted from the tough federal work mandates? The disabled? Mothers with newborns? Victims of domestic violence?

Answering these questions was not easy, for the task force included a diverse group of political voices. On the right were Representative Fran Bradley of Rochester, who argued that Minnesota's package of benefits was so attractive that poor families

Even though MFIP provided broader benefits than AFDC for most welfare families, its passage in 1997 prompted fierce protests at the state capitol because it required work of most adult recipients and adopted the federal five-year limit on cash assistance. Photograph copyright 2002 *Star Tribune/ Minneapolis–St. Paul.*

had little incentive to find work, and Representative Lynda Boudreau of Faribault, who harbored a deep suspicion of the professionals at Human Services and whose work as a home-visit nurse left her convinced that welfare subsidized bad family habits. On the left were Senator Linda Berglin of Minneapolis, a tenacious tactician who wanted broader health and education benefits for poor mothers, and Senator Pat Piper of Austin, a former nun who insisted that almost any investment in Minnesota's children was a good investment.[11]

But the group rather quickly reached consensus on some big questions. They embraced the core element of MFIP, the combination of work mandates and earnings disregards. They agreed that the state would have to put up more money for child-care subsidies, and they said Minnesota should compensate legal immigrants, probably with modest monthly cash payments, for Congress's decision to cut off their food stamps and disability checks. They accepted the federal five-year time limit, arguing that anything less was cruel and unrealistic but that any extension would require the state to put up its own money and undertake substantial fiscal risk.[12]

As the meetings went into February, however, the task force found itself divided. Conservatives argued that MFIP's enforcement policy was toothless: A recipient who defied the state's work requirements could take a 10-percent penalty and continue receiving benefits for months. They noted that other states were using sanctions as high as 100 percent. Representative Lee Greenfield countered that the point of a sanction was not to grind recipients into submission but to demonstrate that the state really was monitoring their behavior. Recipients who didn't play by the rules after several months and several warnings probably had good reason, such as mental illness or poor English literacy, Greenfield argued. Democrats mostly prevailed; the new version of MFIP retained a 10-percent penalty for a family's first violation and added a higher sanction, in the range of 25 to 35 percent, for a second violation.[13]

Republicans also argued that Minnesota had a wildly expansionist definition of work. In its pilot phase, MFIP allowed clients to attend school or job training for up to four years and it counted a variety of other self-improvement measures as "work." Bradley said it was fine for poor parents to attend school, but that the state should expect them to work at the same time. He and Senator Martha Robertson noted that they had hundreds of constituents who were working and going to school simultaneously without a welfare check. Berglin countered that few of those exemplary citizens were single mothers with dysfunctional families and low IQs. But the conservatives held their ground, and a majority formed behind tougher work requirements. The new version of MFIP required recipients to find work within six months or face intervention by county caseworkers, and it permitted only one year of schooling unless a recipient could show in some detail that a degree would lead to higher earnings.[14]

Throughout these debates, however, a centrist political dynamic kept pulling the group back toward the middle. Loren Jennings, who ultimately would carry the bill in the house, represented a large faction of conservative and rural Democrats. Task-force liberals knew that if they drifted too far left, they would lose Jennings and Democrats like him. Senators Sheila Kiscaden and Martha Robertson represented a bloc of moderate Republicans who worried about the hardships facing poor mothers, including violent husbands and troubled children. Task-force hawks saw that a truly coercive bill would stall in the senate.

By the third week of February, as action was picking up in the legislature, the Gang of Twelve had agreed on the rudiments of a bill: time limits, earnings disregards, sanctions, employment and training rules, and benefits for immigrants. Much of the fine print would change again as bills received hearings in the house and senate, but the framework was in place.[15]

But there remained a fiscal backdrop that would bedevil the legislators and Doth's team. The version of MFIP that Minnesota had tested in county field trials was expensive. Because it paid higher benefits and furnished ongoing health insurance, and because it offered extensive job counseling, the pilot version cost about 12 percent more per client than the old AFDC program.[16] As a percentage that sounded small, but it would represent a serious sum in a program that cost on the order of $300 million per year. Although Carlson endorsed the program's philosophy, he remained a budget hawk. When Carlson's Finance Department compiled the administration's overall budget for the coming biennium, it had grim instructions for Doth, Petraborg, and Huskins: the new MFIP had to be budget neutral—that is, it could cost no more than the sum of the new federal block grant and what Minnesota had spent on AFDC in the past.[17]

For weeks, Petraborg and Huskins thought the numbers would never add up. Then they began making a series of excruciating choices. First to go was the "exit level." The MFIP pilot lifted a family to 140 percent of the federal poverty level before easing them off assistance. That was fine when the program was confined to eighty-five hundred families in a handful of counties. Expanded to sixty thousand families in eighty-seven counties, the cost would place MFIP well outside of the Carlson budget allowance. Petraborg, Huskins, and Kvamme ran one computer simulation after another, and ultimately settled on 120 percent of the poverty line as MFIP's new exit threshold. That would still make good on the state's promise to lift families out of poverty, but at a greatly reduced cost.

Next came the budget for case management. Supervising

and counseling poor families, rather than letting them simply collect assistance checks, was labor intensive and costly. Even under the simplified version designed by Kvamme, it imposed new responsibilities on county welfare offices and, during the MFIP pilot, the state had given counties on the order of $3,000 to $4,000 annually per client for administration and employment services. This budget was now cut in half.

Still Doth's team could not make MFIP fit into the administration's budget "box," and so they turned to yet one more cut. It turned out that about one-third of the families receiving cash welfare also lived in subsidized housing. Since they were getting a monthly subsidy that other families were not, Doth's staff proposed counting the housing subsidy as $100 of monthly income and reducing the MFIP grant accordingly. It would save the state something like $40 million in the two-year budget cycle, just enough to make MFIP fit its budget. When word of this proposal leaked outside the department, however, housing advocates and officials at the Minnesota Housing Authority were furious. Advocates noted that subsidized housing was one program with demonstrable results in stabilizing the lives of struggling families and helping them find steady work. Housing officials pointed out that reducing the flow of cash to MFIP families in subsidized housing would also have the effect of cutting their rent payments to public-housing authorities, already badly strapped after federal budget cuts in the 1980s.

By now it was time for crucial decisions in legislative committees, so Huskins assembled her staff once more to review the numbers. They could retreat on the housing proposal. But the only way to save a comparable sum of money was to penalize families who received other federal benefits or jettison the funding for immigrant families who were losing their federal food stamps and disability checks. Huskins, who had gained a reputation for steely resolve under pressure, broke down in tears, but told her aides that the agency would stand behind the housing offset.[18]

These choices not only dismayed the staff at 444 Lafayette Road, they created new frictions with influential members of the religious and nonprofit communities. Brian Rusche, executive director of the Joint Religious Legislative Coalition, warned presciently that cuts in the county case-management budgets would lead to overworked job counselors, making them mere "paper shufflers" rather than effective job coaches. Shawn Fremstad of the Legal Services Advocacy Project warned that many welfare recipients had already tried and failed repeatedly in the job market and were unlikely to do any better if the state foreclosed training and education options.

The weeks of difficult choices, however, seemed to be paying off at the legislature. Democrats who served on the Gang of Twelve felt that a Republican governor had sought their counsel; Republicans felt they were not getting steamrolled by majority Democrats. By early March both houses of the legislature were moving bills through committee and voting on amendments. In the last week of March each chamber passed its own version of the MFIP bill, and by late April a house-senate conference committee had ironed out the differences. On April 28, final legislation cleared the house 120–14 and passed the senate by 67–0.[19] Legislators said they couldn't remember when such a complicated piece of legislation on such a controversial topic had passed with such consensus. MFIP had graduated, rather abruptly and somewhat painfully, from a pilot project to a statewide program for welfare reform.

The choices of the 1997 legislature remained controversial long after the session was gaveled to a close. Poverty advocates and some lawmakers argued that the legislature had vitiated MFIP, abandoning its antipoverty ambitions and turning it into a work-first program rather than a system to advance the long-term prospects of poor families. "We started with a prom dress," Senator Linda Berglin said later, "and we wound up with a house-coat."[20] Welfare scholars such as Gordon Berlin of the Manpower Demonstration Research Corporation argued that lawmakers never really understood the contradiction between the time limits they imposed on cash benefits and the long-term work incentives to which MFIP had aspired.[21] Even among people who followed the Minnesota experiment rather closely there was a feeling that the state had abandoned its principles.

On the question of financial assistance, that critique seems overstated. It is true that the 1997 legislature scaled back MFIP's exit threshold, from 140 percent to 120 percent of the federal

Republican governor Arne Carlson embraced the experiment started under his predecessor, Democrat Rudy Perpich, and signed MFIP into law as a statewide welfare program in the spring of 1997. Shown with Carlson are (from left) Senator Don Samuelson, Senator Sheila Kiscaden, Representative Fran Bradley, Representative Kevin Goodno, Lieutenant Governor Joanne Benson, and Senator Dan Stevens. Photograph copyright 2002 *Star Tribune/* Minneapolis–St. Paul.

poverty line. But it's also true that this remained a big improvement on AFDC, whose benefit structure seldom lifted families above the poverty line, and that Minnesota remained far ahead of other states. Even after 1997, Minnesota ranked number six among the states in its exit threshold—that is, its ability to lift families out of poverty before easing them off assistance.[22] When researchers at the Urban Institute in Washington, D.C., compared the way that all states combined cash benefits with earnings disregards, they found that Minnesota lifted an MFIP family to 120 percent of the federal poverty line while the typical state got its families to just 70 percent of that threshold.[23] It is true that the 1997 legislature narrowed the range of schooling choices available to a parent on MFIP, but it is also true that Minnesota's education and training options after 1997 remained more varied and flexible than those of all but a handful of other states. It is true that the statewide version of MFIP provided counties with less money for job counselors and case managers, but it also true that Minnesota continued to spend more than most states on these services to welfare families.

Last, any survey of overall poverty statistics shows that even after the retrenchment of 1997, Minnesota retained a commitment to poor families that was extraordinary by national standards. It extended child-care subsidies to a far larger group of families than the typical state. (The eligibility cutoff for child-care subsidies was 255 percent of the federal poverty level in Minnesota versus 178 percent nationally.) The same was true for subsidized children's health insurance. (Eligibility reached 275 percent of the federal poverty line in Minnesota versus a national average of 205 percent.)[24] In its 2002 *Kids Count Data Book*, the Annie E. Casey Foundation of Baltimore ranked Minnesota first among the fifty states for child well-being, in large measure because of the health, nutrition, and educational status of its poor children.[25]

That said, the 1997 legislature embraced two elements of the new federal law that introduced troubling and persistent contradictions into MFIP. First was Congress's work-first imperative, the philosophy that getting any job quickly would serve a poor parent better than staying on assistance or pursuing an education. Granted, substantial research supported this approach. A comprehensive national evaluation of welfare-to-work programs carried out for the federal government during the late 1980s and early 1990s found that "labor force attachment" strategies actually outperformed education strategies at raising employment and income for welfare families. They were also vastly cheaper, and so produced a much higher benefit-cost ratio from the perspective of taxpayers.[26] But the same evaluation, and subsequent studies, found that "mixed strategies," those which allowed welfare recipients to combine part-time work and part-time schooling, were the most effective at promoting employment and raising family incomes. In retrospect, it seems clear that the 1997 legislature moved too far toward the work-first strategy, a problem compounded when the Department of Human Services advised counties and local job counselors to emphasize job-hunting rather than school when counseling recipient families. One result was that only about one-fifth of MFIP recipients used any schooling options in the first years after 1997, even though more than one-third lacked a high-school diploma.[27] Another result was that reasonably ambitious, reasonably talented clients—such as Meg of this narrative—felt sometimes at war with their job counselors over their best career options.

A second and more troubling contradiction had to do with time limits. In the original design of MFIP, Joel Kvamme and his colleagues assumed that most recipients would find work after a year or two and leave assistance, but that some families with chronic disadvantages would wash out of the labor market and require public aid indefinitely. They thought it unsurprising and acceptable that some number of disadvantaged parents, perhaps 1 or 2 percent of the adult population, would simply need ongoing aid from the state. Time limits left no room for these families, and the legislature would not address that issue until four years later, and then rather awkwardly. But there was a deeper philosophical conflict between the aspirations of MFIP and the imperative of time limits. Minnesota used earnings disregards to make and keep a promise to poor families: they would always be better off working than relying on welfare. Time limits put an expiration date on that promise. By canceling wage supplements after five years, time limits also clouded the message that job counselors delivered to their clients, an all-important link in the efficacy of a welfare-to-work system. If they were true to the principles of MFIP, local job counselors would encourage their clients to find work quickly and, if necessary, draw a wage supplement from the state. If they were mindful of federal time limits, however, they had to encourage their clients to go off cash assistance as quickly as possible and give up the state's wage supplement. It was a contradiction that left MFIP's admirers deeply troubled.

CHAPTER 7

Real Life, Spring 2002

In the strip mall that adjoins Lucille's school in Brooklyn Park, just across the parking lot and in direct view of a classroom window, is a convenience store called the Speedy Food Stop. It's a regular source of diapers, milk, and cigarettes for the families who live in the apartment complexes across Zane Avenue, and its parking lot serves as a gathering spot where neighbors compare lottery tickets and exchange neighborhood gossip.

On the evening of Friday, April 26, 2002, a twenty-four-year-old customer named Daniel Morrison pulled into the parking lot in front of the Speedy Food Stop, parked his car, and then headed around the corner into a nearby liquor store. There, a cashier remembers, Morrison ran into an old neighborhood rival named Stevens C. Hopson and got into an argument. Morrison left after a few minutes and headed back to his car, but Hopson followed and caught up with him on the sidewalk in front of the Speedy Food Stop. The argument resumed. It turned out that Hopson, fearing a confrontation with Morrison, was carrying a sawed-off shotgun in the athletic bag slung over his shoulder. When Morrison reached into his pocket for car keys, say the police who later reconstructed events, Hopson reached into the athletic bag, aimed it at Morrison, and fired. Morrison reeled from a wound to the chest, then staggered across the parking lot and into the traffic on Zane Avenue. Hopson, who would later plead guilty to second-degree murder, gave chase and fired twice more. Finally, he turned and ran back to the Speedy Food Stop, leaving Morrison to die in the grassy ditch on the far side of the busy boulevard.

Morrison's killing was treated as something of a community tragedy by many of Lucille's neighbors. They erected a small shrine of convenience-store roses in the grass next to Zane Avenue and planted a simple wooden cross bearing the inscription, "D Bubble. We'll miss all the laughs you brought to our lives." One of his girlfriends, a twenty-year-old named Tonya, was a classmate of Lucille at Adult Basic Education and was still mourning his death when class resumed the following Tuesday.

To Lucille, however, the shooting was one more proof that she lived in a neighborhood of fools and reprobates. She had been living in the apartment complex across Zane Avenue for nearly three years. She was tired of the security guards, tired of the noisy parties, tired of the suspicion that her neighbors were drug dealers and gun toters. In her own clipped sentences she makes it plain that she doesn't quite understand what all her adult neighbors are up to, but she knew she could not stay on top of two teenage daughters every minute, and she wanted a safer place.

Even before the convenience-store shooting, Lucille had been thinking about a move. She and the girls shared a one-bedroom apartment, which meant that Lucille slept every night on a couch in the living room and had no good space to do her homework for Adult Basic Education. Now that her girls were teenagers they needed more privacy if they were to have anything approaching a normal social life.

But finding a better home proved daunting. Market rent for

a two-bedroom apartment in the Twin Cities averaged $620 per month at that time, far beyond what Lucille could handle on an MFIP grant of $831 per month. Over the winter she had found one promising apartment for $550 per month. But the landlord also wanted a security deposit of $550. "I ain't got no $1,100," Lucille says flatly.

In March, with help from her job counselor, Patty Czech, Lucille finally qualified for a federal housing subsidy known as Section 8. By the year 2002, Section 8 had become the federal government's biggest housing program for the poor, but it didn't actually build houses or apartments. Instead, it gave Lucille a voucher for use in the private rental market. She would pay 30 percent of her monthly income in rent and the federal government would make up the difference to the landlord. The idea was to get Washington out of building and owning real estate and instead have the government rely on private landlords and market forces. The drawback was that many private landlords refused to partic-ipate. Even though there weren't nearly enough vouchers for eligible families, there were more vouchers than available apart-ments. Just a few years earlier the Family Housing Fund in Min-neapolis had estimated that only one in seven Minnesota families with Section 8 housing vouchers was actually able to secure hous-ing in the private market.[1] Many simply returned their vouchers to the local housing agency in frustration. And that was sympto-matic of the broader shortage of low-cost housing. The Family Housing Fund estimated that the Twin Cities had nearly seventy thousand rental families who earned less than $10,000 a year, but only about thirty thousand apartments with rents affordable at that income.

None of this would have surprised Lucille, who had spent weeks trying to find an apartment she could afford. In late March she found another apartment complex, Ridgebrook Apartments in

Brooklyn Park, that accepted Section 8 vouchers. But it also placed a cap on the number of Section 8 tenants, which meant that Lucille couldn't move in until someone else moved out. Meanwhile, her lease at Huntington Place would expire in June, and then she would either have to move out or sign up for another full year.

Facing this deadline, Lucille became obsessed with finding a new apartment. Since she lacked both a car and a driver's license, this meant long hours on the phone and long trips on city buses to inaccessible apartment complexes, often two or three days a week. It also took a toll on her schoolwork. "It's hard for me to do two different things at once," she says matter-of-factly.

Lucille's struggle to handle two complicated tasks was not lost on Patty Czech, but it didn't surprise her. Four years into the implementation of MFIP, job counselors were discovering that a big share of the welfare population had low IQs and that this limited their ability to handle complicated assignments or juggle multiple tasks. Ramsey County had actually hired a consulting psychologist, Rebecca Glasscock, to evaluate its longer-term welfare clients, and she was finding dozens with IQs that qualified them as borderline retarded. They could hold jobs, as long as the duties were simple and unchanging, but the routine challenges of adult life might well exceed their grasp. "Reading a lease, following a prescription, using a calendar to keep appointments—any one of these tasks might be difficult," Glasscock observed. "And the combination of them might be overwhelming."

In April, Lucille dropped out of school to concentrate on the apartment search. She put the best face on it, insisting she had mastered about as much math and English as she was likely to while sitting in a classroom. And even though the 1997 legislature had tightened MFIP's work rules, the system retained enough flexibility to let Lucille concentrate on housing for a few weeks.

But she also knew that this postponed some important goals, and that her benefit clock was ticking.

The next time I see Meg, in early March, she's at Children's Hospital in downtown St. Paul, and her ambitious trajectory has come to a screeching halt. She hurries into the Ear and Throat Clinic, clutching the baby and trailing the two boys, ten minutes late for a 9:30 appointment. Zachary and Samuel had insisted on stopping in the parking ramp to watch an ambulance helicopter land on the hospital roof and now Meg is afraid that they have missed their appointment. She hurries over to the reception desk, looking slightly frantic, and props the baby on the counter while she checks in with a nurse. Samuel, the four-year-old, skips across the waiting room in his high-top sneakers and winter parka and settles at a play table in one corner. Zachary, seven, still has a tousled, sleepy look, and before long he wanders over to begin needling his little brother and kicking him gently. Soon Samuel is back at his mother's side, taking refuge behind one leg. She brushes Zachary's hair and tells him to leave Samuel alone. The nurse checks a series of documents, then says a doctor will see them shortly. "Boys, come on," Meg says as she scoops up the baby and disappears down a hallway.

When the family emerges from the consulting room twenty minutes later, Meg has a disgusted look on her face. Zachary, who has suffered from periodic sore throats and ear infections since he was a toddler, turns out to have a chronic throat infection. He needs a tonsillectomy. Meanwhile, the doctor has also examined Samuel. The four-year-old has lately developed problems swallowing milk and breathing at night. It turns out that he has an adenoid condition. He too will need surgery.

Meg doesn't know what frustrates her more, that her boys have painful medical conditions that doctors have failed to diagnose until now or that a month of hospital and doctor appointments will derail her plans for job interviews and school applications. She will have to cancel an aptitude test scheduled at St. Paul Technical College two days later because the boys have to come back to the Ear and Throat Clinic. And if the doctors proceed with surgery on both children the next week, she will probably miss an important interview with her job counselor.

"Why does everything happen at once?" she wonders as she begins zipping the baby back into her Snugli. To make matters worse, her car has broken down. She doesn't have $200 to replace the water pump and, rather than tramp around on buses with an infant and two sick boys, she borrows her mother's car every day or two.

Meg's face has grown more pale and a bit puffy in three months, but she retains the same determined look she had at the MFIP orientation where we met. And she still has a trait common to many mothers of small children: she never stops moving.

"Samuel, put your hat on. Zachary, zip your coat up," she says while she finishes bundling up the baby. "We're going to Grandma's." Her mother has agreed to watch the children while Meg sees a guidance counselor at St. Paul Technical College, and Meg is running late.

These childhood medical crises, so familiar to every parent, turn out to be major obstacles in the lives of parents on public assistance. Roughly one-third of America's poor adults have no health insurance, a rate that is three times higher than the national average.[2] As a result, their children are twice as likely to be born with low birth weights and almost three times as likely to have no regular source of medical care.[3]

For affluent two-parent families, a child's illness can be a nuisance and a worry; for poor single parents, it can be an outright disaster. When Zachary or Samuel wakes up with a fever or an earache, Meg has to stay home. Their father still lives in the Twin Cities and sees the children occasionally, but he would laugh out loud if Meg asked him to drive over and stay with the boys while she went to a job interview. If one of the boys needs to stay home from school, Meg stays home. If one of them needs to go to the doctor, Meg goes to the doctor. At the hotel, she missed work at least twice a month because of Zachary's chronic ear infections. Her boss and coworkers were sympathetic, but by her final weeks there her supervisor was warning her that she had to improve her attendance record. Now that she is applying for jobs, she can scarcely mention in a job interview that she will miss work two or three days a month to stay home with sick children. "Well, we'll get through this," she says as they head back to the parking ramp. "We *will* get through this."

Ten days later, Meg is asleep on the living-room couch when I call at two in the afternoon. The boys had come home from surgery the day before and were awake much of the night, first one and then the other, complaining of sore throats and headaches. When she got them back to sleep, the baby would wake up, and soon the baby's crying would wake the boys again. Finally, by early afternoon today, everyone in the house is asleep simultaneously. "Now I know what it's like to have triplets," she says in a tired attempt at humor.

Now, however, Meg has a new set of headaches. She was scheduled to see her job counselor the previous week to discuss her interest in software training. He still wanted her to complete the state's occupational research packet and demonstrate that computer training would actually lead to a better job. Meg had hoped to use her interview to make the case that a computer class at St. Paul Technical College was the right idea.

When she found out that the boys needed surgery, she called her job counselor to reschedule, but he urged her to keep the appointment. As it happened, Children's Hospital scheduled both boys for surgery on the day of the appointment. While the boys were being prepped for surgery, Meg called her job counselor and said she wouldn't be able to make it that day.

"He told me I should come over anyway. He said, 'You'll have an hour or two to kill while they're in surgery.' He threatened to sanction me if I didn't show up. I said, 'I'm not leaving the hospital while my boys are here. If you want to call that a violation of my job plan, then go right ahead. I'm choosing not to deal with you today.'"

Meg and her job counselor eventually resolved the dispute without a sanction—that is, a cut in Meg's welfare benefit—but their battle represents one of the most difficult controversies in the implementation of MFIP and of the welfare-to-work revolution nationally. When Congress passed the Personal Responsibility Act in 1996, antipoverty activists worried about families losing their benefits at the five-year cutoff. But after three or four years, many more families were losing their benefits because of sanctions than because of time limits. This was in part a matter of timing: Most clients in most states didn't hit their time limits until 2001 at the earliest. But it also reflected the important role that financial penalties played in enforcing the nation's new work imperatives. Nationally, 5 to 15 percent of families on assistance were under sanction at any given time, many of them losing a big portion of their welfare grant. In Minnesota the figure was running about 10 percent.[4] Under the version of MFIP approved by the legislature in 1997, Meg could lose 30 percent of her grant— enough to bring her rickety household budget crashing down.

Most state and county authorities agreed that an effective welfare-to-work system needs an enforcement mechanism, given the potential for recipients to cheat the system or merely forget about important appointments. County job counselors across

Minnesota reported in interviews that a certain number of their clients simply wouldn't attend job interviews or keep appointments without the threat of stiff penalties. And some scholarly research found that welfare clients were more likely to participate in job clubs, employment training, and other activities in cities where their behavior was closely monitored.

But sanction research is also highly ambiguous. In states that monitored client behavior closely, there was no evidence that clients who got more sanctions or stiffer penalties actually complied better than clients who did not.[5] Scholarly research also showed that sanctions tended to fall hardest on the most disadvantaged clients—those with little education, poor English, mental illness, or chemical dependency—raising the prospect that it was severe disadvantage, not willful disobedience, that kept welfare parents from complying with the system's rules.[6]

Of greater concern in Meg's case, researchers also found that job counselors sometimes did a poor job of explaining sanction rules and that local counselors had considerable discretion in meting out penalties. As a result, two clients behaving identically might have quite different sanction encounters. In two states, Tennessee and Minnesota, researchers found that one-quarter or more of sanctions were issued in error and reversed on higher review.[7]

Meg understands the issue almost intuitively and, with characteristic pluck, she has substituted her own judgment for that of her job counselor. "I know what he's thinking," she said that afternoon. "I guess a lot of MFIP clients skip their appointments and then blame it on their kids or their doctor. So he's calling my bluff. But I told him that's fine, my kids come first right now."

When I catch up with Patty again, she's out in the garage having a cigarette. She can't shake the addiction, but she doesn't want the townhouse full of smoke when Samantha comes home from school. It seems that March is turning into a rotten month for her too. The manager at Blainebrook Bowl had given her plenty of hours—five nights a week, six hours per shift. But in bartending and cocktail waitressing the income depends on tips, not hours worked. In the weak economy of midwinter 2002, business was not robust at a north suburban recreation center. Many nights she sat idle, making small talk with the other bartenders. Even when there were customers, business was slow and tips were poor. In the last week of February, she quit. "When you're paying a baby-sitter, you can't work for $5 an hour."

Now she has to figure out what to tell her job counselor at Anoka County. He had stressed the importance of finding work quickly and had commended her for finding the Blainebrook job so fast. He generally leaves her alone if she's working and if she calls him with monthly updates. But quitting a job can be a violation of MFIP's work requirements, and now Patty will have to explain her decision to quit what they both thought was a promising job. "I'm just going to have to explain reality to him," Patty says. "I wasn't making enough money to pay a baby-sitter, but I was tied up too many hours to find a better job. Really, they were just tying up my time."

Patty finds herself caught in a puzzle created by many work-first welfare systems. She can find a job easily enough, but the wages are so low that she has to work thirty-five to forty hours a week to bring home an adequate paycheck. This scarcely leaves her time to look after Samantha and keep the household running, never mind looking for a better job or polishing up her old bookkeeping skills. The rules of MFIP would allow Patty to combine work and schooling for thirty-five hours a week. But taking time off for school would mean a cut in take-home pay, and Patty loves having a paycheck. In addition, it would mean finding a bar manager willing to give her flexible hours. It would also require a degree of patience and long-term planning that doesn't come easily to Patty.

The stint at Blainebrook has reminded Patty of another, more nagging dilemma in her life: the conflict between work and her daughter. Samantha's school bus stops along a remote stretch of Coon Rapids Boulevard, and she is the only child to catch the bus there. Just a few months ago, a seventh-grade girl had been raped at a bus stop less than a mile distant, and Patty insists on seeing her daughter on and off the bus every day. Sex is a subject that comes up often in Patty's conversation, often in bawdy, funny stories about one of her girlfriends, but often in a bitter and fearful context. On the matter of Samantha's safety she is adamant, almost obsessive.

Concern for Samantha was one of the factors that pushed Patty toward the bartending job. She knows it sets a bad example for her daughter and that it has no long-term future, but it allows her to be home when Samantha gets back from school and to make sure her daughter has finished her homework and eaten dinner before Patty heads off for work. But for a time, the bartending shifts also meant that Patty had to arrange a nighttime baby-sitter, no easy trick in a far-flung suburb where she knows few of her neighbors. For a few weeks she relied on her landlord's son and daughter-in-law; the couple lived in the adjoining townhouse. The woman was decent enough and was raising two daughters of her own. The son, however, was another matter. Patty often heard him yelling at his daughters on the weekends, often in language that offended even her sophisticated ears. She didn't like the idea that Samantha was at the neighbor's townhouse when the husband might be home.

Patty's child-care dilemma lies at the heart of one of the toughest problems in welfare reform. When Congress passed the

Personal Responsibility Act, some experts predicted that children would suffer as their stressed-out single parents complied with the government's tough new work requirements, while others argued that the children would be better off in high-quality child-care centers than staying home in poor households. Researchers have found that children of poor parents are apt to benefit most from high-quality child care and preschool, where they might be exposed to books, games, and ideas they don't get at home. But researchers have also found that poor families are the least likely to find and use high-quality child care, whether because it is rare in their neighborhoods or because they can't afford it, even with public subsidies.[8] And one of the documented weaknesses in Minnesota's strategy, a trend that would emerge from the county field trials, was that the adolescent children in MFIP families fared poorly in school, compared with youngsters in families on traditional AFDC, apparently because their working parents had less time at home to supervise them.[9]

This is exactly Patty's dilemma. As she moves from one job to the next, she has been able to put together only the most patchy forms of supervision for Samantha. She finally got exasperated with her landlord's daughter-in-law and asked her boyfriend, Don, to watch Samantha at the end of his workday. But this often meant leaving the girl at home alone, playing computer games, for two hours or so between the time Patty leaves for work and the time Don shows up.

On this point Patty envies one of her girlfriends, who also is a single mother but who has parents of her own in the Twin Cities. They help with baby-sitting, they celebrate birthdays with her daughter, and they volunteer to help out in emergencies. Patty's own parents moved to Texas when she was in her twenties and her only brother, her childhood buddy and ally, died in a car crash when they were teenagers. This leaves Patty on her own and dependent on baby-sitters, and that makes her uneasy. "I had my daughter late in life. I'm only going to have one chance to raise her. If I hire the wrong kid to watch her and something goes wrong, who am I going to blame?"

Here too Patty is caught in a contradiction of the new welfare regime. With the Personal Responsibility Act, Congress asked poor single mothers to spend more time at work just at a time when society seemed to decide that parents should spend more time with their children. If she takes a full-time job, Patty will see Samantha only in the evening and on weekends and, worse, have to trust the girl's safety to someone else. If she stays home to see Samantha on and off the school bus, she will doom herself to a dead-end job. In short, she fears being labeled either an inadequate mother or an inadequate breadwinner. She knows that this is the same dilemma faced by millions of other working parents. But she has to solve it alone and with no money. "This is hard," she says, lighting another cigarette. "I never thought I would have to do this on my own."

CHAPTER 8

Making Welfare Work (1998–2000): Minnesota Attracts National Attention

In the spartan little classroom at Lifetrack Resources, JoAnn Brown is back at work on a spring afternoon, this time teaching her monthly job-skills class for MFIP recipients. Four clients had signed up, but two have bowed out because of day-care emergencies. The remaining students are Somali women who sit quietly, shrouded in ankle-length skirts and the head scarves known as hijab.

Brown begins with an audience-participation exercise. She will ask a series of questions, and asks her students to stand if they mean to answer yes.

"Have you ever sent a letter by e-mail?

"Have you ever made a purchase from your living room using the television?"

The point is to demonstrate how technology has pervaded modern life, and how MFIP clients might use it to supplement traditional means of looking for work. Neither of the Somali women stands up.

"Have you ever played a virtual-reality game?" Brown continues.

"Have you ever surfed the Internet?"

Again she draws a blank.

"OK," Brown says without missing a beat, "we'll be teaching you some of this technology as we go along."

Next Brown asks her students to think about job interviews from the employer's point of view. She pulls out a survey conducted by a national research organization. It lists the five top attributes that employers say they want in an employee: honesty, dependability, enthusiasm, flexibility, teamwork.

"Any questions?"

"Yes," one of the women asks softly. "What does that word mean—'enthusiasm'?"

As the Minnesota Family Investment Program began taking root across the state in 1998 and 1999, counties and their employment vendors discovered all manner of mundane obstacles that seldom came up in the political debate over welfare reform but which would prove vexing in the actual task of moving poor adults into the labor market. From Thief River Falls in the northwest to Zumbrota in the southeast, counties had remodeled the infrastructure of welfare. They had merged welfare departments with employment offices; they had drawn up scripts for MFIP orientation class; they had retrained caseworkers to make them job counselors; they had formed partnerships with local employers that were likely to hire low-skilled workers. And in the first two years after MFIP went statewide, about one-third of its clients were making the transition to work quickly and easily. Most of them had job experience and marketable skills, and had merely found themselves knocked out of the workforce by a domestic crisis, a medical emergency, or a layoff. Once the county had helped them leave a violent partner, survive an eviction, arrange medical care, or resolve some other temporary crisis, they stepped back into the job market and found work.

But a second tier of the caseload was struggling. These

clients were cooperating—they were meeting their job counselors, typing up their résumés, scheduling job interviews—but
they faced a variety of minor roadblocks. For most clients these
barriers were so ordinary that they seldom commanded attention
in the political arena: poor literacy, for example, or the lack of
a driver's license. But they were enough to scare off some employers or to rule out a big share of available jobs. Other clients
simply lacked the ordinary luxuries—a reliable car or a helpful
neighbor—that enable typical working parents to survive small family emergencies and continue getting to work dependably. These
handicaps weren't particularly dramatic, but they were stubborn
and widespread, and they were enough to explain why so many
welfare recipients wash out of their jobs after a few weeks and,
indeed, why they wind up on public assistance in the first place.

When Wilder Research Center, a branch of St. Paul's Wilder
Foundation, surveyed MFIP recipients who were struggling to
find work after several months, the chief barriers were surpris-
ingly ordinary and yet quite vexing: poor English skills, unreliable
cars, a shortage of evening and nighttime child care.[1]

Even an employer who is desperate for workers or eager to
demonstrate good corporate citizenship might give up on an
employee who misses work without notice for three days in a row,
or who routinely shows up thirty minutes after the assembly line
starts rolling, or who tells a supervisor, "Well, you're just going to
have to deal with my attitude today."

When Wilder's researchers surveyed employers who had
hired welfare recipients in the early days of MFIP, they heard a
range of comments that was frank and not especially sympathetic.
"Some of these single moms don't know how to juggle work and
home life," said one employer. "They don't understand about
being on time, every day—basic commonsense things," said
another. "The primary problem is work ethic. They just don't

want to work," said a third. "It's not our job," said a fourth. "It's the government's."[2]

To bridge this gap between employer expectations and client assets, the counties began improvising. And so, at sunrise one morning along Lake Street in south Minneapolis, a half dozen urban commuters are waiting for their morning bus to the suburbs. At 5:45 A.M., bus No. 681, the "Earlybird," comes barreling down Interstate-35W and pulls onto the elevated ramp. The sleepy riders climb aboard, find seats, and settle in for the twenty-minute ride to distant Eden Prairie.

The Earlybird is one of endless improvisations that Minnesota counties started making as they labored to get welfare clients to work. Hennepin County discovered that a large share of its poorest families were clustered in inner-city neighborhoods and lacked reliable cars, while many of its most promising employers were spread out along suburban freeways or in remote greenfield industrial parks. These employers were desperate for workers in the booming economy of the late 1990s, but they were virtually inaccessible by public transit, especially for a single parent who might need to get home quickly for a family emergency in the middle of the day. So in 1999, Hennepin County contracted with South West Metro Transit, a suburban bus line, to run a reverse-commute service that would deliver urban adults to far suburban employers every morning and back to the city again at night.

Not that the Earlybird made life a cakewalk. On this particular morning Bill Newcomb, a single father with a son in junior high school, rose at 4:30 to prepare for his day at a bill-collection agency in Eden Prairie. He packed a lunch for himself and one for his son, reset the alarm clock so that his teenager would wake for the school bus, and was out the door by 5:15 for a fifteen-minute walk to the bus stop. He'll call the house by cell phone at 7:45 to

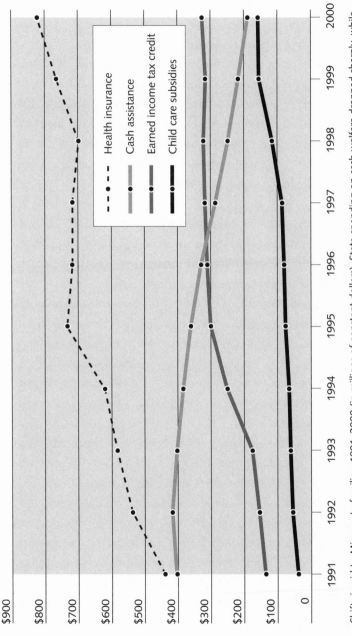

Shifts in aid to Minnesota families, 1991–2000 (in millions of constant dollars). State spending on cash welfare dropped sharply, while outlays for work supports such as child care, subsidized health insurance, and employment tax credits rose substantially. The new mix reflected a migration of Minnesota families from welfare to work and an increase in state supports for the working poor.

make sure his son is up, pray that the cell phone doesn't ring again with some emergency before his workday ends at 4:00, and then begin the sixty-minute commute back home.

At 6:20 A.M., as the sky is turning pink in the east, the Early-bird pulls into a Park and Ride lot off the highway in Eden Prairie. Three riders disembark and board a smaller Dial-a-Ride van that will carry them into the warren of office buildings and industrial parks that sprawl across this growing suburb. Three others stay onboard for even more remote jobs. They have made the leap from welfare to work, but just barely.

In the early years of MFIP, during the field trials, counties received substantial sums from the state to hire job counselors, provide short-term training, and then provide continued coaching for clients who struggled in the workplace. In the leaner statewide version created by the legislature in 1997, counties and their contracting agencies got less money for these employment services, roughly $1,000 to $2,000 per client per year. The practical result was that job counselors saw their caseloads double or triple, to one hundred clients or more, and that many recipients got little more from their counselors than a monthly phone call and a bus pass.

During these years MFIP clients and their advocates reported a troubling inconsistency in the quality of job counselors. Some of the Hennepin County and Ramsey County vendors, such as Hired and Lifetrack Resources, hired job counselors with advanced degrees, set aside large budgets for training and tuition, and instructed their staff in the nuances of diagnosing domestic violence and chemical dependency. In other places, clients reported that their job counselors couldn't explain the most basic rules of MFIP or understand the local bus system. The same Wilder Research team that heard employers grumbling about MFIP clients also detected dissatisfaction among employers and local nonprofits with the quality of job counseling offered by the counties and their contractors. "County workers are not always able to identify clients' barriers at the first assessment," one survey respondent said. "Caseloads are too high," said another. "The work-first focus is pushing too many people into lousy low-wage jobs," said a third.[3]

Still, the state was pouring money into work services for MFIP clients. Between 1996 and 2000, the share of Minnesota's welfare expenditures that went into direct cash assistance dropped from 70 percent of total outlays to 43 percent. Meanwhile, the share going into employment services doubled, from 5 percent to 10 percent, and the share going into child-care subsidies for working clients tripled, from 12 percent to 36 percent.[4]

Counties weren't the only ones to recognize that MFIP would need partners in the employment transaction. In 1997 the McKnight Foundation, Minnesota's largest philanthropic organization, provided $20 million in grants to cities and counties that formed community partnerships tailored to local welfare-to-work needs. The initial round of grants lasted for only two years, but they spawned twenty-two experiments affecting eighty-six counties and funded popular services such as low-cost car loans and training for child-care workers.[5]

The irony was that, by 1998 or 1999, many in Congress and the Minnesota legislature regarded welfare reform as a finished task since they had written, debated, and passed legislation. On the ground in the county welfare offices, however, local authorities were just beginning to work out the kinks and discover what actually worked with troubled clients and skeptical employers.

In the spring of 2000, when the Minnesota Family Investment Program was beginning to take hold as the state's new welfare system, Joel Kvamme got a long-awaited phone call from New York. Evaluators at the Manpower Demonstration Research Corporation had finished their review of the MFIP pilot project and were ready to present the findings to the Minnesota authorities. The Department of Human Services notified legislators, advocates, practitioners, and journalists, and on May 31, a team of four MDRC evaluators arrived in St. Paul for a daylong series of briefings, seminars, and news conferences.

By this time, the MDRC findings were in one sense moot. The pilot version of MFIP had expired when the county field trials came to an end, and Minnesota had been operating a scaled-down version of the program statewide for more than two years. No one could promise that results from the county field trials would hold true in the more austere statewide version of MFIP, and it seemed unlikely that the legislature would ever revert to the earlier pilot version. Nevertheless, the MDRC findings are worth considering in some detail. They created a sensation in the national research community, and, because of MDRC's intricate research design, they reveal in great detail the strengths and flaws of financial incentives and work mandates in welfare reform.

Minnesota had asked its evaluators to answer a long set of questions about MFIP's performance. Some of these would be of interest to welfare reformers anywhere: Did the program increase employment among welfare recipients? Did it reduce dependency? Was it cost effective? A second set of questions addressed Minnesota's peculiar aspirations: Did the new approach raise family incomes? Did it lift clients out of poverty? Did it improve the stability of the families and the well-being of the children?

To answer these questions, the evaluators used the gold standard of social-science research, a random-assignment experiment that divided their sample of 14,639 welfare families by lottery, with half going into MFIP and half into AFDC. Researchers could track two parallel cohorts of families in comparable circumstances and ask if a change in welfare rules and services made any difference in their lives. But the researchers also subdivided the sample families into various subgroups—long-term recipients versus recent applicants, for example, and single-parent families versus two-parent households. Each of these groups brought different characteristics to the welfare system, and each was subject to a different set of benefits and rules in MFIP.

Of greatest interest were single-parent, long-term welfare recipients. These cases represented perhaps half of the welfare caseload at any given time, and they animated the stereotypes of legislators and taxpayers. They were also the clients who had failed in one welfare-to-work strategy after another over the years. And in the MFIP pilot, they also received the most powerful set of services. They got financial rewards for taking jobs, in the form of higher benefits and wage supplements from the earnings disregard. But they were also subject to "mandatory employment services"; that is, they had to report to a job counselor every month and document their search for work. As it happened, this group was also MFIP's biggest success story. At the end of the three-year research period, the evaluators found that their employment rates were much higher than those of the AFDC control group (49.9 percent versus 36.9 percent), and their earnings were 23 percent higher. Plainly, something in the combination of work incentives and work mandates had made a big difference in this group's behavior.[6]

For single parents who were new to welfare, the results were more modest. This group received MFIP's financial rewards for taking jobs, but they were not subject to mandatory job counseling. Here again, the MFIP group had higher employment rates after three years, but the gap was slim: 55 percent for the MFIP sample as against 52 percent for those assigned to AFDC. Because typical welfare applicants had always achieved relatively high employment rates as they left welfare, there wasn't a lot of room for improvement in this group. In this sample, however, the MFIP group did not have higher earnings than the AFDC group. Apparently they were able to work fewer hours, or accept jobs at lower wages, because they were receiving a partial welfare benefit after finding work that the control group did not receive.[7]

For two-parent families, the results were again slightly different. The MFIP sample was about as likely to be working as the AFDC sample, but these families too had lower earnings than their AFDC counterparts. The researchers surmised that these couples had higher total incomes because of a more generous MFIP cash benefit, and so made the decision that one partner would work less and stay home more.[8]

As for MFIP's second goal, reducing poverty, the results were encouraging across the board. Among both new applicants and long-term recipients, the MFIP group had higher incomes and lower poverty rates than the AFDC group. Long-term recipients in MFIP, who had higher earnings and higher government benefits than their AFDC counterparts, had total incomes fully 15 percent higher than those in the control group. New applicants in MFIP, who had higher benefits but not higher earnings, were about 8 percent better off than their counterparts in AFDC.[9]

With respect to dependence on government aid, the findings were mixed. MFIP clients, both new applicants and long-term recipients, were slightly more likely to be drawing welfare benefits after three years than their counterparts in AFDC. That's because MFIP allowed them to keep a partial benefit after they found work, while the AFDC recipients quickly lost their benefits. But the MFIP clients were much *less* likely to rely solely on government aid for their income. That's because most of them had found work and were combining a paycheck with a welfare check.[10]

It was when the evaluators got to nonfinancial impacts, however, that they produced their most striking results. The Minnesota team had asked MDRC to examine several indicators of family well-being; these were deemed vital goals of an antipoverty program, but they were also notoriously resistant to government interference. By the day of the Minnesota briefing, these results were not entirely a surprise; the organization had previewed them to an advisory panel that included prestigious scholars such as Robert Solow, the economist and Nobel laureate at MIT, and Henry Aaron, a respected labor economist at the Brookings Institution in Washington, D.C., and they had created a buzz in the research community. Nonetheless, the results were stunning. MFIP seemed to produce higher marriage rates among two-parent and single-parent families, a result that appeared unprecedented in welfare-reform experiments. In addition, long-term recipients reported sharply lower levels of domestic violence and abuse, an issue that was drawing more and more attention from poverty researchers. And they reported better school performance and fewer behavioral problems for their children.

These striking results weren't uniform across the subgroups, and they had some troubling exceptions. Parents of adolescents, for example, reported more behavioral problems among their children as they spent more time at work. Still, they were the broadest range of improvements in family well-being that the MDRC staff had measured in any welfare-to-work program, and the evaluators made it plain that they thought they had groundbreaking research.[11]

The sobering side was that achieving these results wasn't cheap. MFIP wound up spending about 12 percent more on each family than the traditional welfare system, or $47,000 over a three-year period compared with $42,000 in AFDC. This mostly reflected higher cash benefits and continued health-insurance subsidies for families who found work, though some of it reflected the higher costs of job counseling and employment services to MFIP clients. But the Minnesotans had expected higher costs going into the experiment and concluded that stable families with better jobs would justify the word "investment" in MFIP's acronym.

As researchers pored over the findings, they drew several conclusions about the Minnesota design. First was that a combination of financial incentives and work mandates could succeed even with the toughest clients—long-term, single-parent recipients who had resisted most previous reform efforts. For these recipients, MFIP produced a sharp increase in employment and a dramatic increase in earnings. They were slightly more likely to be drawing a government benefit than the AFDC sample, but they were much more likely to be working and much less likely to depend solely on government aid for their income. After three years in MFIP, they were working their way out of poverty, and their families seemed to be better off as a result.

Second was that welfare reform might indeed achieve some of the social intangibles sought by liberals and conservatives: higher marriage rates, stable families, thriving children. Although the exact causation remained something of a mystery, the evaluators were able to conclude that MFIP produced these impacts where it delivered higher family incomes as well as an increase in employment.

Yet MFIP also had a weakness, and it revived the old contradiction between assisting families and promoting self-reliance. MFIP recipients who were not subject to firm work requirements—mostly new applicants—didn't increase their work effort as much as their counterparts in the traditional welfare system. These families apparently used their additional cash benefits as a substitute for earned income and either worked fewer hours or accepted jobs at lower wages than their counterparts in the less generous AFDC program. Minnesota had succeeded in raising their household incomes, but very possibly it had allowed them to work less than they might otherwise have. Social scientists called this effect the "leaky bucket": an additional dollar spent on a government program would not yield a full dollar in higher family income if the recipient chose to use government aid as a substitute for earnings rather than a supplement to earnings.

But even here, there were consolations in the MDRC report. Among the families who produced the leaky-bucket effect, it appeared that recipients were using government aid to reduce family stress. In two-parent households, one spouse was working slightly less and spending more time with the children. In single-parent households, recipients were buying better child care and paying for additional extracurricular activities for their children. In effect, the MDRC team said, Minnesota was "purchasing" higher family well-being.

Last, in a nuance that would prove highly influential in the research community, the MDRC report suggested how the government might plug the leaky bucket. For the subgroup of families consisting of long-term, single-parent recipients, there was no leak in MFIP. These clients, who were subject to tough work requirements in addition to new financial rewards, showed such strong increases in work and earnings that every additional dollar of MFIP benefits yielded almost exactly a dollar of higher family income. This was unusual, set against the cost-benefit analyses of previous welfare-to-work programs. It was this combination of work incentives and work mandates that might allow the government to achieve its two much-desired goals: less poverty and more work.

As the year 2000 drew to a close, counties and their vendors were gaining more experience with MFIP and its clients, and their counseling strategies grew more sophisticated. Before long, the most talented MFIP counselors were not just experts in the local job market but guides who could initiate their clients into the mysteries and intricacies of work.

While most MFIP recipients did possess some work experience, about a third had essentially none. They were mostly young mothers who had become pregnant as teenagers and stayed home to raise children. About one-fifth of the recipients had themselves grown up in welfare households and had no experience of a working adult in the family. These clients represented a peculiar challenge—bright, often personable and talented, but deeply alienated by experience, trust, and sometimes race from the American economic mainstream.

Clients like these became a specialty of Christopher Stewart, a job counselor at Jewish Family Service of St. Paul, one of the nonprofit agencies that provided employment counseling to MFIP clients in Ramsey County. At the agency's pristine offices on West Seventh Street in St. Paul, Stewart is greeting the six students in his Challenge Group one morning in January. The six adults are recent MFIP applicants—four single mothers, all African American, and two single fathers, one black, one white. All six have been out of work for months or have only the most sporadic work history. Challenge Group is designed to teach the "soft skills" of employment—punctuality, congeniality, dependability—and to give the six clients moral support in the difficult task of looking for work. This morning's topic is time management.

"Some of you folks have been out of the paid workforce for a while," Stewart begins. He has an easy charm that allows him to be frank with his clients without giving offense. "I know it's easy to let time slip. You're supposed to meet a pal at ten o'clock but maybe you show up at eleven instead. Well, I'm here to tell you that that won't cut it in the job market. Time is money. People who don't understand that become annoying real fast.

"Now, my schedule, I'm booked by half-hour increments. If you're supposed to see me at ten o'clock and you show up at 10:20, you throw off my whole schedule. Then what do I do with the next person I'm supposed to see?"

He hands out monthly planning calendars. At last week's meeting, everyone had penned in his or her goals for the month. A young woman across from Stewart volunteers what she has written down: "Clear my credit rating. Find child care. Begin job search."

"Great," he says. "Now look over your calendar for next week so I can schedule individual appointments with each of you. This time next week, you should be farther along on your plan than you are today. I want you to understand that feeling—that feeling that you're making progress against your plan."

He gives the group a few minutes to list goals and consult their calendars

"Now, I know some of you are getting pretty busy these days, what with finding child care and setting up job interviews and seeing me. Before you go to bed at night, how many of you kind of see the next day in your head and plan it out, A-B-C-D?"

There are one or two nods.

"OK, how many of you write it down on paper? You know, a schedule for the day?"

Not a hand goes up.

"OK, let's say you've got a job interview at two this afternoon, and at eight o'clock your daughter is sick and can't go to daycare. What would you do?"

There is a long silence. Finally Mike, sitting in one corner, raises his hand cautiously. "I'd call them later on, when my daughter is better, and see if I could reschedule."

"Good idea," Stewart replies. "But it would be an even better idea to call them *before* the appointment. Warn them that you're going to miss it. If you just don't show up, then call them later to reschedule, that's trouble. An employer is going to think, if this guy doesn't have the skills to make a job interview on time, he sure doesn't have the skills to hold the job."

Next Stewart wants to discuss communication. He distributes a handout that lists listening skills such as "Stop talking. You cannot listen if you are talking," and "Show that you want to listen. Look and act interested."

He reviews the importance of listening carefully to a job interviewer or a supervisor on a new job. Then he turns to language skills. "One trick I've found in my career is that you have to learn the language of the company where you're working. Every workplace has its own language, and you should know that when you're applying for a job. If it's an insurance company, they'll have certain concepts and kinds of language that they use. If it's a computer company, it will be something else. Every workplace has its own language, and that is going to be the language of success."

A hand goes up across the table from Stewart. It's Luverne, who is black and just moved to Minnesota from South Carolina. "You mean don't use Ebonics, right?" she says. "You mean talk white."

Stewart chuckles, then turns serious. "OK," he says after a pause. "This gets us into some pretty heavy issues. But let's go ahead and talk about them.

"I used to work for an insurance company, doing customer service by telephone, and I got real good at disguising where I'm from and who I am. I got so good at it that a few times I had people who didn't know I was black, and you wouldn't believe the things they'd start saying to me. There were a lot of days when I had to bite my tongue because I knew that speaking my mind was not going to be consistent with professionalism in the customer-service area. But it was not easy.

"I've been in Minnesota for a long time now, and I've learned to talk in a way that, on the telephone, people can't tell who I am or where I'm from. But when I go home to New Orleans, my sisters call their friends over. They sit me down and say, 'OK, say something,' and then laugh because they think I sound funny."

"Yeah," Luverne says. "If I go out to a job interview and talk the way I talked around my family in South Carolina, people up here can't understand me. I'm like, whoa, this is a really different place."

"OK," Stewart says, "But let me be clear about this. This isn't about speaking the right way or the wrong way. Most people in Minnesota don't speak the queen's English. Everyone has a home language, the language they speak at home. That includes white people in Minnesota. But the people who make it in life leave that home language at home. At work they use the language of work, the language of money."

"Yeah, but people around here, they have accents too," Luverne says.

"You bet they do. I call it Scandi-sotan. So I'm not asking you to talk white or talk black. I'm asking you to use the language of money. This is the language that will put gas in your car, food on your shelf, and money in your pocket."

Christopher Stewart's class notwithstanding, anyone who observed MFIP in action during its first three years had to conclude that its implementation was rushed and imperfect. Job counselors were plainly overworked, and their quality was uneven. An applicant showing up for welfare orientation one morning in one county might get a lucid and upbeat introduction, while an applicant somewhere else might get a lecture that was listless and opaque. Some job counselors knew local employers intimately;

others seemed content to refer their clients to the nearest convenience store for a cashier's job. Some job counselors monitored every move of every client; others felt powerless to discipline the clients who were gaming the system.

And yet the new strategy seemed to be working. A decade earlier, in February 1991, Joel Kvamme's design team had produced a memo titled "Why MFIP?" to explain their proposal to legislators and federal regulators. The memo set out a series of goals they hoped the new strategy would achieve. Among the targets: 37 percent of MFIP clients would be working at any given point, 44 percent of long-term recipients would find work in a timely fashion, and 77 percent of MFIP families would see higher incomes.[12]

Now, nearly ten years later, MFIP was exceeding every goal. A report issued by the Department of Human Services in December 2000, surveying both new MFIP applicants and long-term recipients, found that 60 percent of each sample was working and many had left assistance entirely. Recent applicants had doubled their incomes since entering the program; long-term recipients had raised their incomes by a fourth during the twelve months covered by the survey. By late 2000 recipients in both samples were working enough that, on average, they relied on public assistance for less than one-fifth of their income.[13]

If critics found a flaw in MFIP, and they did, it was that Minnesota's approach was slow to cut caseloads. Reducing welfare rolls had become a headline measure of success in the welfare revolution, in part because the federal government required states to report caseloads annually and in part because caseload reduction was a simple measure easily grasped by the public. Between August 1996 and September 2001, Minnesota's welfare caseload fell by 31 percent, while the nation's fell on average by 52 percent.[14]

But caseload reduction is a misleading measure of MFIP's

success. Because Minnesota deliberately allowed recipients to keep a portion of their welfare grant after they started working, it had to count thousands of families who had found jobs, were receiving only nominal benefits, and would have been off the caseload in most other states. If authorities had subtracted MFIP recipients who were working nearly full-time in the year 2000, a group that would have been off assistance in many other states, the MFIP caseload would have dropped by an additional 20 percent.[15]

A more useful set of questions asks what happens to recipients as they move through the welfare system: How quickly do they find work? Are they better off after they get jobs? Can they stay off assistance once they leave? On these measures Minnesota's performance was stronger and, indeed, as strong as that of any other state. Among applicants who entered the program in MFIP's early months, for example, fully 70 percent were off assistance again in less than two years.[16] The share of MFIP recipients who held jobs upon leaving assistance, steadily 80 percent or higher, was also above the national average. And the average family that left MFIP was living well above the federal poverty line, a performance that also exceeded national averages.[17]

In the matter of cutting caseloads, MFIP inevitably invited comparison with Wisconsin, a state that became famous for its disappearing welfare families. The comparison is natural, for the two states have similar populations and political traditions and yet adopted radically different strategies toward welfare reform. During the period that Minnesota cut its welfare rolls by 31 percent, Wisconsin reduced its caseloads by a stunning 64 percent. By the year 2000, welfare hawks in Minnesota had begun to argue that their state was too lenient.

Yet the outcomes of MFIP and W-2 were more similar than commonly thought. One reason for Wisconsin's dramatic caseload decline is that the state simply removed several thousand "child-only" cases (typically cases where an eligible child was living with grandparents or other relatives) from its welfare-to-work head count and shifted them to a different state program. Another reason is that welfare recipients deemed "employable" by local job counselors in Wisconsin were also moved off of cash assistance, whether or not they actually found work. If Minnesota's caseload were adjusted for these subgroups, its caseload would have fallen by 60 percent, against 64 percent in Wisconsin, over the same period.[18]

When MFIP and W-2 are compared on comparable terms—that is, in their ability to accept clients and move them quickly into jobs—MFIP often outperformed the Wisconsin program. About two years after MFIP took effect statewide, the Minnesota Department of Human Services examined comparable samples of welfare recipients in Milwaukee County and the Twin Cities. Researchers found that after one year in the new employment programs, the Minnesota and Wisconsin cohorts were equally likely to be working and that the Minnesota sample was actually slightly less dependent on public assistance.[19]

As for family well-being, the ultimate goal set out by MFIP's creators some years earlier, Minnesota was outperforming essentially all its peers. When legislative auditor James Nobles examined the status of MFIP families and MFIP leavers in early 2002, he found that the share of MFIP alumni who had escaped poverty was well above the average for comparable states and nearly twice as high as in Wisconsin.[20]

In short, despite the bumpy ride of its early implementation, MFIP was outperforming its predecessor and, apparently, its counterparts in most other states.

CHAPTER 9

Real Life, Summer 2002

It's a few weeks after Mother's Day, in the early summer of 2002, when I see Patty again, and she has another patented story of familial discord. She and Samantha spent Mother's Day weekend at Don's lake cabin and arrived home Monday morning to find a thick packet of legal documents from Anoka County. It was a series of letters and contracts spelling out the county's plan to collect Patty's child-support payments from Samantha's father.

"I'm reading through these, getting more excited by the minute, when the phone rings. It's him, of course. He got the same packet in the mail and he's scared as hell. He wants to know if he can start sending me a little cash every week or settle this without signing a bunch of papers. I told him no way. I can get in trouble with the county if I don't cooperate—and he owes us the money anyway.

"Then he starts in with the whining. His truck broke down. He can't get to work. He doesn't have the money for a new transmission. I said, 'Wait a minute, where were you when my truck broke down? Where were you when I was out of work? Where were you when I was going to get evicted? In case you've forgotten, it's Mother's Day! I don't have to listen to this!'"

Patty's little victory on the child-support front is just one of many auspicious signs as spring unfolds.

"I got a new job," she announces, fussing with her cigarette lighter. It's another bartending job, but one with a better pedigree. It's a supper club at a suburban golf course. Two of her girlfriends have worked there; they vouch for the manager and report that the customers are good tippers. With warm weather finally on the way, she expects the place to be packed with happy golfers. Even the hours are good, falling on prime shifts: Wednesday, Friday, and Saturday, 5:00 P.M. until midnight. "Three nights a week is enough, if you get enough hours and the tips are good," she says.

In addition to this break, Patty has cooked up a little entrepreneurial scheme with one of her girlfriends. Visiting a favorite bar one night, they noticed that two of the waitresses were selling girlie calendars that featured themselves dressed in skimpy shorts and halter tops posing on farm implements. The bar owner had loaned them the money for printing, and they collected a share of the proceeds for every calendar they could sell at local bars. Patty has a friend who sidelines in photography, and she knows any number of bar owners in the Twin Cities suburbs. She reckons that she and her friend could produce a calendar of their own with a motorcycle theme. Granted, she's thirty-eight years old, not eighteen, but she's still proud of her body and doesn't mind posing in a bikini. "We could sell a million of those," she says.

Between the new bartending job and some freelance bookkeeping, Patty is putting in at least thirty hours a week, which means that she has qualified for the McKnight Foundation's interest-free car loan. This saddles her with a monthly car payment, but it gives her great satisfaction to own the Camaro she had been borrowing from Don—and it means that, if her relationship with Don breaks off, she at least has her own source of transportation.

How long Patty can juggle all these projects isn't clear. Nor has Patty quite figured out her long-term career plan. But her job counselor seems content to leave her alone as long as she is working and filing monthly job logs. As a newcomer to MFIP she still has more than four years of benefits in the bank, and it's too early for her or her job counselor to panic. "As long as I check in with him once a month and give him someone who can verify that I'm working, he doesn't climb down my throat. He's more like a support group than a boss."

But the best news is that Patty and Don have decided to get married. "I've never been happier in a relationship," she says in a way that seems heartfelt but also slightly desperate. Despite more than her share of bad experiences with boyfriends, Patty still likes having a man in her life. "I love every minute I spend with Samantha, but, you know, you need a little adult action too once in a while. And it's nice to know that somebody thinks you're not over the hill yet."

The relationship with Don introduces some tensions into life around Patty's townhouse. Samantha isn't sure about the new man in her mother's life, especially when he tries to play surrogate father. Patty says that Don's presence often brings out the insolent side of her daughter. Samantha understands that her own father is no great role model, but she seems to resent another adult with his own set of expectations. Then, too, Don is going through a separation of his own, and his soon-to-be-ex-wife makes regular calls to his cell phone, with plenty of editorial comment about Patty.

But a steady relationship also introduces an important element of stability into Patty's life. Don, who has two teenage sons of his own, has agreed to watch Samantha on the three nights when Patty works at the golf course. She knows him well enough now to trust him with her daughter, and this gets her out of using her noisy neighbors as baby-sitters. She and Don also are talking about moving in together. His mother is getting ready to vacate a nearby townhouse—much bigger and nicer than the one that Patty rents—and it would save her $400 a month in rent, a staggering sum in her budget. Then there are also more routine matters such as transportation. When the Camaro breaks down, Don can fix it or lend her his car. "When you have as much car trouble as I do, you need a backup," she says, although it's not clear if she's referring to Don or his vehicles.

In seeking an emotional and financial partner, Patty is more typical than she knows. Although the Personal Responsibility Act assumed that most welfare parents would find jobs and earn their way off assistance, scholars found that a substantial number of recipients left assistance through marriage, or at least through cohabiting with someone who had income. In one influential study, Harvard economists Mary Jo Bane and David Ellwood found that nearly 30 percent of all "exits" from welfare occurred when a female head of household found a steady partner with enough income to lift the family off assistance.[1] This would have come as no surprise to Joel Kvamme, who had observed years earlier that, starting in the late 1970s, most American households relied on two paychecks to attain middle-class comfort.

The need for economic partnerships is even more crucial in the low end of the job market, where workers like Patty are unlikely to earn more than $15,000 per year, or roughly the poverty line for a family of three in 2002, and are vulnerable to frequent layoffs. From the earliest days of their work together, Kvamme and his colleagues had conceived of MFIP as a sort of economic partner to impoverished single parents, a way for them to stabilize their lives after a divorce or separation until they could start their lives over again, financially and emotionally.

On a rainy afternoon in July, Lucille is due at the Hired office in Brooklyn Park to see her job counselor and update her employment plan. This afternoon she'll see Simone Reiss, who has taken her case while Patty Czech is on maternity leave. The Hired office sits at the back of a remote office park, which means that Lucille has had to beg a ride from a friend with a car, and she's in a hurry when she ducks in out of the downpour.

The interview begins with good news: Lucille has found a new place to live, a two-bedroom apartment in a complex that accepts Section 8 vouchers. It's not perfect—her daughters complain that their bedroom is cramped—but it's a good deal bigger than her apartment at Huntington Place and it's on a bus line that runs past her school. Reiss congratulates her. But the apartment search had qualified as an MFIP job-related activity for the summer, and now Lucille needs a new employment plan to meet the program's rules. Reiss asks if Lucille is ready to go back to school.

It develops that there is a new complication in Lucille's life. Her mother, a chronic diabetes patient, has to enter the hospital for a possible foot amputation. She has asked Lucille to come down to Mississippi for the month of August to look after her. Lucille's three brothers live nearby, but all three have full-time jobs and families of their own. Besides, Lucille's mother wants a daughter there to help with tasks such as bathing and dressing. "I'm her baby," Lucille says. "She and I have always been real close."

This means postponing school yet again and Lucille is plainly frustrated. Lucille keeps her sentences short and her emotions close, but her disappointment is clear. "It's hard. You need a good education to get anywhere, and I just don't have that," she says. Nevertheless, she has decided that family duty comes first, and she plans to board the Greyhound bus in two weeks.

In making this decision, Lucille captures another of the frictions created by welfare reform. Even in an era when most women work, the United States has retained the vestiges of an older division of labor, an arrangement where men are the primary wage earners and women are the primary caregivers. This helps explain why men spend so much less time on family responsibilities, or even in community service, and why women chronically earn less than men, even in comparable jobs. Many Americans chafe at this division, but in households with two spouses, most families arrive at their own balance. In households headed by single parents, however, the juggling act can be overwhelming. And welfare reform, by placing new demands on recipients, often forces poor single parents into vexing choices between their obligations to the family and the demands of the state.

Though she frames it in the sparest phrases, Lucille confesses she is torn by the dilemma. She recognizes that, as a matter of rational calculation, she should stay in Brooklyn Park and finish school. It is required by MFIP's rules and it would greatly improve her prospects in the job market. Yet as a matter of family duty and social well-being, she should drop out and go to Mississippi. There is a public benefit—it will save taxpayers some of the expense of her mother's care—and there is a pull of family obligation that she cannot defy.

Simone Reiss sympathizes with Lucille's decision. But she also warns that MFIP requires Lucille to put in the requisite number of hours on some sort of self-sufficiency plan. She and her colleagues at Hired also are mindful that Lucille has reached her forty-seventh month on federal benefits, and they're beginning to worry that she won't be prepared to support herself in another year when her cash benefits run out. So this afternoon Reiss reminds Lucille of a third option: applying for a federal disability program called Supplemental Security Income. Congress created the program in 1972 for poor adults who are blind, disabled, or elderly. It provides a monthly check, something over $500 per month in 2002, for an adult who falls below a certain income threshold and is demonstrably unemployable. The Social Security Administration, which administers the program, still encourages recipients to look for work and aim for self-reliance, but unlike welfare in the post-1996 era, SSI does not have a fixed time limit or rigid work requirements. Minnesota, like many states, has begun encouraging local welfare job counselors to consider SSI as an alternative for their clients when there is clear evidence of a disability, and every year since MFIP started in 1998, several hundred MFIP families had made the conversion to SSI. Lucille had submitted an application some weeks earlier, and now she must decide whether to continue with it.

Reiss and Lucille discuss the possibility, and Lucille decides she wants to make the application. It's a bit humiliating, because it means admitting to her own cognitive and physical shortcomings, and it says tacitly that she has less confidence in her ability to find work. But she is utterly honest about her own intellectual difficulties and, mindful of the time limit on federal benefits, she is worried foremost about supporting her daughters if her welfare benefits run out.

Summer has turned into a time of struggle for Meg too, and she is fuming when I talk to her in mid-July. On the previous night, St. Paul police officers had come upon one of her neighbors dealing drugs in the little parking lot behind her apartment house. When the suspect's partner ran inside, police officers gave chase and proceeded to search the building door to door. At 10:30, she awoke to the commotion out back and heard pounding on her door. Much to her relief it was a police officer, not a fugitive drug dealer, standing there when she opened the door a crack. Still, the episode kept her building in an uproar for an hour and Meg didn't get back to sleep until after midnight.

The neighborhood that Meg chose when her marriage broke up, St. Paul's East Side, is not a high-crime area. With typical diligence she chose a respectable place, a neighborhood built around a sprawling 3M Company factory and the old Hamm's Brewery. It's a neighborhood of up-down duplexes and immaculate bungalows, and in the 1950s it was St. Paul's emblem of blue-collar pride. With the decline of St. Paul's manufacturing economy in the 1980s, the East Side lost many of its white ethnic factory workers and attracted a large population of working-class Hispanic and Hmong immigrant families. But it remained tidy and mostly safe.

Still, living on less than $1,000 per month, Meg simply could not afford a spiffier neighborhood and she fretted about small things, such as letting her boys play in the grassy strip beside their apartment house. Her building had been the scene of a drive-by shooting in late winter and a murder a year earlier. After the drug bust she was fed up and determined to find a new neighborhood. But she faced much the same challenge as Lucille. Only Meg wasn't yet qualified for Section 8 housing; she was on the waiting list and couldn't hope to get a voucher for at least eighteen months.

Meg finishes the police story and then, with evident satisfaction, announces she has landed a job. In April, once Samuel and Zachary had recovered from surgery, Meg finally had the freedom to start looking for work in earnest. This meant that she qualified for child-care subsidies from the county, which in turn gave her the time to polish her résumé and schedule frequent job interviews. Her mother had been watching the children occasionally through the winter and agreed to take on full-time baby-sitting. To Meg this was much preferable to finding some stranger to watch her children, but she hadn't felt she could ask her mother to take on full-time day care without payment. Meanwhile, Lifetrack had assigned her to a new, more compatible job counselor. He too discouraged her from enrolling in school full-time, but he urged her to look at jobs carefully and take one that would offer rewarding work and the potential for advancement. Finally—children healthy, child-care arranged, bills paid—Meg felt she had a stable foundation to start anew.

In May she phoned an agency called Top Temporary. She described her clerical experience and filled out an application. Two days later the agency found her an assignment reading proofs at a printing company. A similar assignment with a real-estate brokerage followed two weeks later and then, in early June, a receptionist job at a bank three miles from her house. She felt she was settling for second best, because she still had her eye on some sort of computer training or health-care certification. Still, she took the job seriously and asked her supervisor if she might apply for something permanent. She found the bank interesting and knew there was the prospect of a promotion. It also paid well, $10 per hour at thirty-five hours per week. This was enough income for Meg to go off the cash portion of her MFIP benefit and collect only food assistance and health insurance. She had long since settled on this as a strategy because it would stop the ticking of her five-year benefit clock. Finally, the job's hours were good. "It's no weekends and it means we can eat dinner together," she says with a satisfied sigh. "For now, that's good."

This would have been the perfect time for her ex-husband, Anthony, to rejoin the picture and give Meg some financial support. Since she is off the cash portion of MFIP, she would be able to keep any child-support payments he made. But Anthony has disappeared. This too had been a bureaucratic struggle for Meg. In her first months on MFIP, she resisted filling out all the paperwork required for the state to pursue a child-support order. She and Anthony were fighting over his rights to see the children, and she simply didn't want him around. Then the county threatened to sanction her, and she filed the paperwork. Anthony made a few child-support payments, and even offered to pay the lump sum required to catch up with his child-support back orders. But if Meg had collected that sum, it would have put her over the asset limit to qualify for MFIP and its other benefits. Then, in June, Anthony's payments simply stopped entirely. Meg heard through a mutual friend that Anthony had given up on life in the United States and had returned to Brazil. About this she has mixed feelings.

"It would be nice to have some money from him, but I don't want him in my life anymore. He's the one who got me in this mess in the first place."

CHAPTER 10

The Limits of Welfare Reform (2000–2001): When Work Isn't the Answer

Cindy Widman slips behind the wheel of her white Nissan Sentra and pulls out of the parking lot at Jewish Family Service of St. Paul. A vocational counselor serving Ramsey County recipients of Minnesota Family Investment Program benefits, Widman works with the most fragile and struggling clients—adults who can't balance a checkbook, can't read a bus schedule, can't even get out of bed on some mornings. Most of her clients are so shattered or disorganized they cannot reliably keep a biweekly appointment at her office. So she goes to them.

The client this morning is Dolores, a thirty-six-year-old single mother who lives with her ten-year-old son in a shabby neighborhood on St. Paul's north end. Her case file shows that Dolores started drinking at age sixteen and was an alcoholic by age twenty. She has been sober for three years—she says voices told her that alcohol would kill her—and she has moved out of the drug-ridden neighborhood of Minneapolis where she grew up. But she hasn't been able to hold even simple jobs, such as stocking shelves at Kmart or working as a cook's assistant. Now she has reached her fifty-first month on assistance and is in danger of exhausting her federal cash benefits.

While more typical MFIP clients like Meg, Patty, and Lucille are making gradual progress toward their goals, a smaller group that includes clients like Dolores, perhaps a quarter of the state's caseload, cannot seem to gain any traction whatsoever. They are variously known as the disadvantaged clients, or the "hard to serve," and in the late 1990s they emerged as perhaps the most vexing challenge in a welfare-to-work system.

We arrive at Dolores's house, a miniature Victorian painted pastel pink and divided into up-down duplex apartments. Plastic sheeting flaps from the front porch windows—cheap insulation against a Minnesota winter—and a sagging set of wooden steps leads to the front door. Dolores greets us meekly at the top of an interior flight of stairs and welcomes us into the apartment. The living room is spotless—the brown shag carpet is freshly vacuumed, the windows sparkle against the winter sun. But the room is strangely empty. Although Dolores and her son have lived here for three months, they have no furniture. Red and blue bath towels hang in the windows in place of curtains; a lone mattress covers the floor of the front bedroom. The only furnishings in the living room are a compact stereo cabinet and a big Panasonic television set. To compose poetry, her current hobby, Dolores sits on the floor and writes at a cardboard box.

"Good morning," Widman says warmly. "It looks like you haven't used the furniture voucher I gave you last month."

"Oh, I haven't gotten around to that," Dolores replies softly. "They extended it for another month." This troubles Widman. She has been encouraging Dolores to take more initiative in the organization of her life. But she understands: using the voucher would mean taking a bus across town before 8:00 A.M. to the Catholic Charities furniture warehouse, waiting in a long line of applicants, and then having to spend $20 in cash to pay for a van to haul the new furnishings back to her neighborhood.

Dolores is as tidy as the apartment. Her sleek black hair is pulled back in a clasp and she has donned a flowered print blouse over bright purple stretch pants. But she has a distracted air as she invites Widman into the kitchen. This room too is spotless and scrubbed, but nearly as bare as the living room. A battered round Formica table and three chairs sit before a sunny window, but the only furnishing is a coffeemaker that sits on a kitchen chair against one wall. A few photographs of Dolores's son and mother are the only personal effects.

Dolores holds a license as a nursing attendant, a degree that would qualify her for work and good wages at any one of many Twin Cities nursing homes. But she has resisted Widman's suggestion that she take on a full-time nursing home job. She says it would be too stressful, and a visitor soon begins to understand why. Dolores's hands flutter anxiously above her lap as she speaks and her eyes flit around the room. Her conversation drifts from one topic to another; a sentence that begins with details of her new job winds up describing her passion for poetry, and more than once she stands up in midsentence to wander out of the room.

Dolores is working as a domestic aide for an elderly woman at a high-rise residence two miles away. She visits every day for two hours to cook and tidy up. Widman found the agency that employs her, a company called TLC, Inc., then drove her to the job interview and to the preemployment physical exam. She couldn't run the risk that Dolores would forget any one of these appointments, or simply suffer an anxiety attack and refuse to leave home. Now Widman's goal is to find out whether Dolores can take on a little more work.

"How's it going with this client?" she asks.

"I like her," Dolores answers. "She likes me. It's rewarding. It makes me feel like I'm doing something for someone."

"Good, good," Widman replies. "But you know, we need to

start increasing your hours. That's important for meeting the guidelines of the program, and it might qualify you for an extension when your benefits run out. What do you think about talking to TLC and asking for another client or two?"

"I probably will take on more hours," Dolores says carefully. "I'm starting to get behind on my bills." She gazes out the window. "But I was sort of waiting for TLC to give me more hours. I'm just waiting . . . waiting."

Widman pauses. "Dolores, I'd like to see you have a little more direction. You know, not just wait for things to happen to you."

"I know," Dolores replies. "But sometimes I feel that if I direct myself, I'm just going to walk into a wall, and then I'll have to start off in another direction. I'd rather have the Creator guide me."

Widman pauses again. "Where do you go to see this client?"

"It's called Hamline Towers. It's a high-rise."

"Are there other clients there?"

"Probably. They've got seventeen floors."

"I mean, does TLC have other clients in that building that you could work for?" Widman is hoping that Dolores can find additional clients in the same building. Combining a few jobs at one site would save Dolores many hours of commuting by bus to other jobs, not to mention the anxiety of tackling a strange new workplace.

"Oh, yeah, there's one woman who already asked me if I could help her out too."

"Perfect, perfect!" Widman says.

She makes a note to call TLC when she gets back to her office. Then she asks about Dolores's poetry, an avocation that plainly brings out her initiative and self-confidence.

"I've been on the Internet, talking to some poetry teachers.

I found a place that said they would take some of my poems. That's how I would really like to make my living."

"Do they purchase poems?"

"Well, I don't know. I didn't ask that."

"You know, Dolores, sometimes we have to do work that pays money in addition to what we want to do."

"What I'd like to do is get my poems framed, and then sell them at art fairs and festivals."

Widman makes another note to contact Women Venture, a St. Paul nonprofit that advises women on starting their own businesses. Even if Dolores cannot actually earn a living by writing poetry, she could make some money framing and selling her poems. It also would bring some organization and satisfaction to her life, and it might count as work hours to qualify Dolores for extended MFIP benefits.

"OK, Dolores. Thank you for seeing us," Widman says. "I'll talk to TLC about some more clients for you, and I'll get you some information about Women Venture. It sounds like things are coming along just fine."

With that the interview is over. Widman makes a final note to herself: if Dolores does not pick up extra clients and hours at the Hamline high-rise, Widman will order a psychological assessment to see if she belongs in a government disability program rather than on welfare. Widman packs up her briefcase, gives Dolores a warm handshake, then descends into the bright March sunshine.

A client like Dolores—with her anxiety disorder, wandering mind, and occasional hallucinations—is not what the general public associates with the term "welfare mother." But welfare scholars and county caseworkers have always known that the system was full of these shattered souls.

In the old welfare system, the AFDC program that operated

from 1935 to 1996, such clients were largely invisible. If they filed an application and met the eligibility guidelines—generally, if they were single parents and extremely poor—they could stay home and collect a monthly check until their children grew up. In Ramsey County, some veterans dubbed the system "feed and forget."

But in the new landscape created by the Personal Responsibility Act, such clients suddenly came into plain view. They were expected to go out and find work, and if they hadn't succeeded within a year or so, an inquiring caseworker had to find out why.

Welfare scholars soon began examining the medical and cognitive traits of welfare recipients, and what they found confirmed the impressions of veteran caseworkers. In an influential study published by the University of Michigan, sociologist Sandra Danziger and a team of researchers studied a large sample of representative welfare recipients and found that 35 percent had diagnosable mental illnesses (three times the rate as in the general population) and 20 percent had children who were disabled or chronically ill (twice the rate of the general population). In addition, 15 percent or more had been victims of domestic violence (four to five times the rate of the general public) and 47 percent lacked a car or a driver's license (six times the rate of the general public).[1] Studies by the Urban Institute in Washington, D.C., and by Lifetrack Resources in St. Paul had found similar handicaps among long-term recipients.

Such adults challenge the premise of MFIP, which assumed that most clients would respond rationally to simple work mandates and financial incentives. And they shatter the assumptions behind the Personal Responsibility Act, which supposed that the great majority of welfare adults simply lacked the gumption or motivation to go out and find work. "They don't need more rules and more authority figures," says Cindy Widman. "If rules and authority worked for them, they would have succeeded a long time ago."

Mental disorders aren't the only barriers that test the premises of a welfare-to-work system. In the same week that Widman was visiting Dolores, across town at another employment-services agency called Hired, a counseling supervisor named Barb Dahl had just finished interviews with two long-term recipients. One was a twenty-five-year-old mother with an IQ of seventy. By itself, low intelligence is not an insurmountable barrier to work. But it is often associated with impulsive behavior, and this client had three young children by three different fathers and two convictions for drug possession. Ordinarily Dahl would have tried to find her a job in banking, retailing, or a nursing home, three industries with frequent openings for women with modest skills. But in Minnesota all three industries now routinely conducted criminal background checks on job applicants. Dahl was trying to get the drug convictions expunged from this client's court record, then discovered that she had been recently charged again, this time for child neglect because she left her ten-year-old in charge of the two younger children while she went to the neighbor's apartment for a visit. "Employers used to cut applicants some slack when the job market was tight," she says. "Now they have plenty of applicants without felony records."

Dahl's second client was a single mother in her late thirties with a normal IQ and a respectable résumé. But she also had a fourteen-year-old son with borderline retardation and a violent temper. In October, the client was fired from her job cashiering at a SuperAmerica gas station after missing work for the fourth time to take her son out of school. It was his third fight in a month, and she was spending many hours at the school counselor's office. Now, after two months looking for a new job, she was facing eviction from her two-bedroom apartment in Brooklyn Center. The neighbors alleged that her son had bullied their children, and one had threatened to call the police. Rather than try to mollify three angry families, the landlord had chosen to evict Barb's client.

"Do you know what it's going to take to get her another apartment?" Dahl asks, rubbing her temples. "Most landlords won't rent to a tenant who's unemployed. What's she going to put on the lease application?" And yet, unless Dahl could help this client find a new apartment, she would be filing her next round of job applications from a homeless shelter.

Disadvantages like these—a disabled child, a low IQ—are not uncommon in the general population and don't by themselves bar a motivated adult from holding a job. Indeed, lawmakers and governors have struggled to say who should be exempt from the work requirements of the new federal system, precisely because many adults with mental and physical disabilities do perfectly well in the workplace.

In the toughest welfare clients, however, these barriers tend to cluster in groups of three and four. And while any one barrier might not stop a client from working, the combination of several can be crippling. In Danziger's study, for example, more than one-third of the surveyed welfare recipients had two to three barriers, and nearly one-fourth had a combination of four to six. "Lack of a high-school diploma by itself does not constitute a rigid barrier to employment," Danziger's team wrote, almost as if they were thinking of Barb Dahl's first client. "But an employer might be less willing to hire a high-school dropout who also has few work skills, transportation problems, and is chronically depressed."[2]

These difficult cases started coming to Minnesota's attention in late 1999. Many clients had embraced the work message of the new system. Most were writing résumés and attending job clubs. In the booming economy of the late 1990s, many clients were finding jobs quickly and moving off assistance.

But then there was the stubborn third—the clients who even after eighteen months of incentives from the state and coaching from job counselors still had not found work, despite the strongest job market in memory. Now these clients were closing in on the five-year time limit imposed by federal law, and counties hadn't done much for them. Plainly, these clients were going to need more than a bus pass, a fresh résumé, and a monthly phone call from their job counselor.

By late 1999 county welfare directors began complaining to Chuck Johnson, who had risen from a staff position on Joel Kvamme's research team to become MFIP director at the Minnesota Department of Human Services. Some urged the state to simply release whole categories of clients from federal and state work requirements; the Personal Responsibility Act allowed each state to exempt up to 20 percent of its caseload from the federal five-year time limit on assistance. Johnson and leading members of the legislature resisted, arguing that no one could predict categorically who was capable of work and who was not. Instead, Johnson proposed a way to bolster county services to the troubled clients. Three years after the passage of the Personal Responsibility Act, many states had surplus funds in their federal welfare accounts because their caseloads had fallen rapidly while their federal grants remained fixed. Minnesota was no exception. At the suggestion of Monty Martin, director of Human Services in Ramsey County, and his peers from other counties, Johnson proposed creating new pools of money the state could hand out to counties for use at their discretion in serving the more challenged clients. Johnson's proposal for these "Local Intervention Grants" won the approval of a new governor, Independent Jesse Ventura, and for a second time in its fifteen-year history, MFIP survived a change of political administrations. In the spring of 2000, the Minnesota legislature approved a $75 million package to bolster MFIP, including one-time grants that counties might use on intensive services, such as home visits and psychological assessments of troubled clients.

County welfare directors were delighted with the intervention grants, not only because they provided extra money but also because they could be adapted to local needs. Rice County in south-central Minnesota, trying to integrate a growing number of Somali and Mexican immigrants into an overwhelmingly white community, hired a social worker to advise its MFIP caseworkers and clients. Sprawling Otter Tail County in west-central Minnesota experimented with sheltered-workshop jobs and home visits to reclusive clients.

Many counties used the money to create teams of intensive case managers with small caseloads and advanced skills. Where a typical MFIP job counselor might work with ninety to one hundred families at a time, scarcely talking with each client once a month, the new intensive case-management counselors would handle just twenty or thirty clients and see each of them every week or two. The counselors would also come with special qualifications—a degree in vocational rehabilitation, for example, or social work. This is how Cindy Widman came to be an intensive case manager in Ramsey County's MFIP program.

When a new case file arrives on Widman's desk, it seldom reveals much except that the client has been looking for work unsuccessfully for three or four years. In the work-first strategy adopted by most states and generally by Minnesota after 1996, few clients received thorough IQ testing or psychological screening when they entered the welfare system. Most counties instead administered a simple test of basic math and vocabulary skills at the client's orientation session and then supplied the test results to the client's job counselor. Moreover, job counselors found that many clients deliberately hid their disabilities; they might have

lingered on the margins of society for years without telling anyone they could not read or suffered from hallucinations. Minnesota was not unusual in failing to detect such barriers early. A
report by the U.S. General Accounting Office in March 2001
found that most counties in most states relied on client self-
disclosure or the most primitive screening tools when applicants
first entered the welfare-to-work system and that severe barriers
such as mental illness and learning disabilities often escaped the
notice of local job counselors.[3]

When Widman makes a house call, she has a variety of tech-
niques to aid her own diagnosis. She will produce some important
document, then hand it to the client upside down. If the client
scans it and hands it back, she is reasonably sure he is hiding illit-
eracy. On the pretense of pointing to a clock or a photograph, she
will swing her hand past the client's face. If she cringes or cowers,
Widman knows there's a good chance of domestic violence in her
past. Widman estimates that a third of her clients at any given
time are borderline retarded, a quarter have a diagnosable mental
illness, and one or two are homeless.

By the middle of 2001, counties had put together a battery
of tools to help such clients. In Ramsey County, Widman could
refer them to licensed psychologists to see if they had diagnosable
mental impairments that might exempt them from federal time
limits. Those with disabling illnesses or severely ill children might
apply for Supplemental Security Income. Those who seemed com-
pliant and motivated but badly disadvantaged might take tran-
sitional jobs at Goodwill or Packaging First, where work sites
formerly known as sheltered workshops offered paid jobs under
close and supportive supervision.

The Local Intervention Grants greatly extended MFIP's
range of services and triggered resourceful responses to daunting
client problems. But to the frustration of many county welfare

directors and job counselors, the strenuous new county efforts didn't reach many MFIP clients until 2001 or 2002, when many had already exhausted three or four years of cash benefits. Again, Minnesota was not alone in this belated response. The General Accounting Office surveyed six states in 2001 and found that none of them were collecting caseload data on the incidence of mental illness or drug abuse, and that none were making "informed programmatic decisions" about how to serve such troubled clients. The GAO recommended that federal authorities encourage states to do a better job of assessing their welfare clients and remind states of the flexibility allowed under federal law to meet recipients' diverse needs.[4] In Minnesota, where the data and the problems were beginning to emerge, the frustration was nonetheless palpable. "We should have had those grants from the beginning," said Jane Samargia, executive director of Hired. "Some of our clients were just marking time for three years because no one had the time to spot their needs."

With a degree in vocational rehabilitation, Widman insists that she can guide any client into some form of rewarding work. Whether these clients will ever hold steady jobs and support their families, however, is quite another matter.

Joel Kvamme, John Petraborg, and the other creators of MFIP had anticipated that there would be such clients. In Kvamme's original conception, MFIP would use the labor market to sort clients and assess their abilities. Those who had vocational skills, good health, and reasonably stable emotional lives would find work without much help from the state and move off assistance rather quickly. Those who struggled in the job market would come under the supervision of a county caseworker and get help digging up employment leads and polishing their job-hunting skills. But Kvamme and Petraborg, who both had worked in county welfare offices, knew there would be clients who could not find or hold a job even after two or three years of assiduous effort. They expected the number to be small, but they also deemed it acceptable that any state at any time would have a few thousand families who simply could not make it by their own efforts and needed indefinite public aid.

But Kvamme and Petraborg were designing MFIP before the Personal Responsibility Act of 1996, with its demanding work requirements and five-year cap on cash benefits. The authors of the federal law also anticipated there would be clients who could not meet the statute's ambitious work targets. They created a hardship set-aside, allowing each state to exempt 20 percent of its caseload from the five-year time limit. But the 20-percent figure was derived from political negotiation in Congress, not from research on the actual characteristics of the welfare caseload, and as states such as Minnesota began to understand their welfare populations better, it was not clear that 20 percent would suffice. "It seems likely that the share of families requiring long-term cash assistance will exceed the federal 20-percent exemption, at least in some states," wrote Sheila Zedlewski and Pamela Loprest of the Urban Institute in Washington, D.C., which was conducting the nation's most comprehensive survey of poor families on and off assistance. "This will certainly be true if jobs become scarcer, especially for those with limited education and health challenges. We do not know to what extent employment barriers can be overcome with the right combination of services and case management."[5]

By early 2001, Chuck Johnson and county welfare directors were starting to worry about the twin problems of time limits and clients who could not hold jobs. The easy clients were finding work and leaving MFIP, pushed off by the program's strong work message or pulled off by the strong job market. Many of the remaining clients were either so underskilled or so saddled with emotional and medical problems that employers shied away from them. The first of Minnesota's MFIP families would hit their federal time limits in July 2002. Many of them, the counties feared, would look like Dolores.

Early in 2001, Governor Jesse Ventura's administration drew up a compromise to address the time-limit problem: Minnesota would extend the benefits, at state cost, of any family that hit its five-year time limit while making a good-faith effort to comply with MFIP's rules. But the state would also grant counties authority to impose stiffer penalties, including a 100-percent grant reduction, on any recipient who defied the rules. Michael O'Keefe, Ventura's commissioner of Human Services and former executive director of the McKnight Foundation, argued that the threat of early, heavy penalties would motivate MFIP clients who really could hold jobs—reducing the number who ultimately hit their time limits—while benefit extensions would cover clients who really could not.

The Ventura proposal went over well with Democrats in the Minnesota senate, although some balked at the 100-percent sanction. In the GOP-controlled house, however, the plan met stiff resistance. House Republicans feared that the O'Keefe rule would create a loophole for permissive county welfare workers to extend client benefits and, in effect, repeal the very concept of time limits. They proposed a much narrower rule: the state would extend benefits, but only for recipients who were genuinely unemployable and only upon certification by a doctor or vocational specialist.

At the Department of Human Services, Chuck Johnson, who was trying to find a middle ground between Democrats and Republicans, feared that the house plan was too narrow. His statistics showed that a large share of the families approaching their time limits were not strictly unemployable. In fact, they were working, but earning such low wages that they could not lift their families out of poverty and off MFIP. Cutting off their benefits after five years would in effect penalize some of the families who were trying hardest to comply.

For perhaps the first time since MFIP's creation, the dispute over time limits pushed the legislature toward a partisan deadlock. The senate passed one version of extensions, the house passed another, and by late spring the issue was stuck in a house-senate conference committee. For much of MFIP's history, social liberals had held substantial leverage in the legislature. From 1987 until 1998, Democrats held majorities in both chambers, giving them huge control over committee business and floor votes. Even when they couldn't hold their conservative colleagues, progressives such as Lee Greenfield and Linda Berglin managed through sheer expertise or technical acumen to craft the fine points of poverty legislation. Now, however, they were stuck. If the conference committee couldn't strike a compromise acceptable to conservative house Republicans, the legislature would adjourn without any language to avert time limits, and hundreds of families would start exhausting their benefits the following year.

Representative Kevin Goodno, now a leader in the Republican caucus and the party's chief welfare expert, was under pressure to retain the conservative social message in welfare reform. But Berglin held her ground, and the conference committee ultimately adopted three extensions. The first two, reflecting the Republican point of view, created hardship extensions. They covered MFIP recipients who were "hard to employ" as certified by a vocational expert, or who were chronically ill, certified to have an incapacitating injury, or were needed at home to care for an ill or incapacitated child or relative. The third, a nod toward the Democrats' position, granted benefit extensions to parents who were making a good-faith effort to work but remained too poor to leave assistance. But the rule set a high standard for "good faith" effort: thirty hours per week of work and work activities for single parents and fifty-five hours per week for families with two parents.

The three extension categories proved an acceptable compromise at the state capitol, but they turned out to be laborious and costly for the counties. By early 2002, Ramsey County had more than four hundred families approaching time limits on July 1; in Hennepin County the figure was nearly six hundred. Between them, the two big metropolitan counties had about three-fourths of the Minnesota MFIP recipients expected to hit time limits in 2002. Because the recipients had such complicated problems, and because the consequences of terminating their grants were so grave, both counties set up elaborate screening processes. In Ramsey County, employment-services vendors such as Lifetrack Resources and Jewish Family Service conducted face-to-face interviews with clients approaching their time limits, but could also refer them to clinical psychologists and vocational therapists for detailed assessments. In Hennepin County, a job counselor would review the recipient's case file, then accompany her to a meeting with four or five top county specialists. These "exit interviews" proved cumbersome and time consuming, in part because the clients' cases were so complicated and in part because the clients were so disorganized and fearful that they often failed to show up.

The cases crossing Barb Dahl's desk at Hired in the spring of 2002 illustrated the excruciating decisions that counties would have to make if they intended to protect the most vulnerable recipients without abandoning the work imperatives of MFIP. One such client was Deborah, a thirty-six-year-old single mother with five children and an IQ of seventy-two. She was working thirty-five hours a week at a bill-collection agency, but she wasn't earning enough money to lift her family off assistance. Before the exit interview, her job counselor had pored over her case file, now as thick as a phone book, to review her work history, family circumstances, housing situation, and physical and intellectual abilities. Then Deborah, the job counselor, and Dahl drove to Hennepin County Government Center in downtown Minneapolis for Deborah's exit interview. The county team explained the federal law on time limits. They described the government benefits that Deborah could continue receiving after July, probably Medicaid and food stamps, and explained how she could appeal the county's decision to terminate her benefits. They asked if she understood the consequences of losing cash assistance, and what she might do as a result.

They also explained that Deborah might qualify for a benefit extension under one or more of the legislature's categories. With an IQ of seventy-two, Deborah almost certainly could have qualified under the hard-to-employ extension. Even the federal government, with notoriously strict rules for the Supplemental Security Income program, set the disability threshold in many cases at an IQ of seventy. But Deborah was, after all, working quite successfully. And more to the point, Dahl reported that Deborah was so proud of her job that no one in the county welfare system wanted to tell her that her she will go down in the books as "unemployable." Deborah could also have qualified for the state's good-faith effort extension, since she was working thirty-five hours a week. But her job counselor pointed out that Deborah could lose her job at any time. She had lost eight other jobs in the previous five years, which didn't seem surprising for a woman with five young children and poor organizational skills. And if she lost her job at the bill-collection agency, she would also lose her state extension and her benefits. In the end, after a brief conversation, Dahl and the job counselor decided to propose

Deborah for an exemption on the grounds of her low IQ, and they hoped the county approved.

As Hennepin and Ramsey County authorities interviewed clients such as Deborah, they confirmed the suspicion that many of the recipients facing time limits were the same deeply disadvantaged adults they had begun to worry about one year earlier. Statistics compiled by Chuck Johnson's office showed that, compared with the general MFIP population, recipients closing in on time limits were more likely to be immigrants, especially immigrants with language problems and large families, to have extremely poor educational credentials, and to be well into their thirties, which suggested chronic physical or emotional problems.

Ramsey County came to a similar conclusion. Clinical psychologist Rebecca Glasscock, on loan from the county's mental-health division, was screening time-limit MFIP recipients and finding that these adults were more like the county's mental-health caseload than like the typical welfare population. Of the first ninety-one time-limit clients she screened during the early spring of 2002, roughly one-fourth were illiterate in English, three-quarters had disabled children, and more than half had IQs below eighty. Among this group, she reported, were adults who couldn't recall their own addresses, couldn't plan their schedule more than one day in advance, and couldn't remember to change their clothes at night. The chief difference between them and adults in the county's regular mental-health population, Glasscock observed, was that they had grown up in poor families and poor neighborhoods, and no one had caught their cognitive impairments until they foundered in a welfare-to-work system.[6]

As if the five-year deadline weren't pressing enough, employment counselors and their clients found themselves up against a deteriorating job market. Many states had noticed an economic slump starting in the spring of 2001, and the terrorist calamity of

September 11 had pushed the nation into a genuine recession. Between March 2001 and March 2002 Minnesota's unemployment rate jumped by a full percentage point to 4.3 percent. That remained low by national standards, but it meant that job creation had ground to a halt. The state economy, which had created some forty thousand new jobs every year through most of the 1990s, had suddenly lost almost thirty-seven thousand jobs in the previous twelve months. And yet county welfare officials were still expected to push another fifteen hundred welfare clients into the labor market every month.

At the county welfare offices and nonprofit vendors such as Hired, the collision of recession and time limits introduced a new level of tension. At Jewish Family Service, job counselors wondered out loud if clients would blame them when their benefits were cut off, and the agency planned a new paging code for counselors who feared confrontations with clients. At Lifetrack Resources, each job counselor was given a security beeper to summon help from colleagues if a client threatened violence. At Hennepin County's central office, a psychologist warned that the children of one client wanted to wait outside the room when their mother went through her exit interview; they were afraid she might turn violent in such a confrontation.

As it happened, July 1 came and went without a major humanitarian crisis for MFIP families. Housing advocates reported no surge in evictions, homeless shelters reported no spike in applications, food shelves reported no wave of needy families. This may have reflected a simple matter of timing: most families wouldn't be evicted in their first month without cash, and many MFIP recipients would have had some spare resources or relatives to tide them over. But it also reflected the fact that the number of families who actually hit their time limits was much smaller than anyone had expected. The Department of Human Services had predicted two years earlier that several thousand families might hit their time limit as early as July 2002. But on July 1, the number reaching sixty months was only about nine hundred. And because counties applied the state extension categories aggressively, about two-thirds of these families received benefit extensions.[7]

But even if Minnesota averted a crisis that many had expected, the twin challenges of time limits and disadvantaged clients left several residual problems. First, long-term recipients were likely to accumulate in the system over time. Even though just six hundred families were granted extensions in July 2002, the state expected another four hundred or so families to hit their time limits in every subsequent month. Because these clients were by definition adults with the biggest barriers to work, they were likely to stay in the system and represent an ever-growing share of the caseload. The second problem was cost. Granting extended benefits to troubled clients averted the counties' nightmare—that is, indigent families with no source of support—and prevented destitution for these troubled adults. But it meant that they would continue to draw benefits at state expense. And while the state could use federal funds from the welfare block grant to pay benefits to these families as long as they remained less than 20 percent of the state's caseload, it was not clear how long that would last.

Last, the summer of 2002 raised the broader social question of what society expects from its most disadvantaged citizens. One could argue that the Personal Responsibility Act did the nation a favor by forcing communities to take a good close look at their most troubled families. In this, as scholars and job counselors discovered, it shattered the myth that most long-term welfare recipients were simply willful malingerers. But the law did not really settle the question of what society owed a single parent who, through physical disability or mental impairment, could not really hold competitive employment.

Screening clients for benefit extensions certainly forced counties to probe this question more deeply; some insisted that recipients on extended benefits remain with their job counselors and continue the search for work; others were ready to deem the recipients simply unemployable. Ramsey County, for example, didn't have enough money to send every long-term recipient to a vocational specialist or a supported-work agency such as Goodwill. But it wasn't willing to give up on them either. Deborah Schlick, who oversaw the extension process in Ramsey County and made a close study of the most troubled families, found the decisions agonizing. "Here's a single mother with five children, diabetes, and low IQ," Schlick observed one day that summer. "Do I send her to SSI and take away her job counselor? Isn't that sort of giving up on her?"

Having exposed these families, welfare reform has in a sense called its own bluff. If voters really believe that essentially all adults should work, then they will have to support the costly and labor-intensive case-management system that helps an illiterate father fill out a job application and gets a paranoid-depressive mother out of the house every morning. Conversely, if voters accept that their communities contain some small number of adults who simply cannot support themselves and their children without public aid, then they will have to accept the relaxation of work requirements and time limits. As the new era of welfare reform reached its sixth year, it was not clear whether the general public had grasped this choice and would rise to the challenge of helping deeply disadvantaged adults or would revert to an earlier habit of pretending they do not exist.

CHAPTER 11

Real Life, Fall 2002

Lucille is sitting in the Social Security Administration field office in downtown Minneapolis, waiting for her SSI appeals hearing to start in twenty minutes. She's looking elegant in a navy blue suit, conservative pumps, and a modest shade of red lipstick, but she has tucked herself away in one corner, and the look on her face says she would bolt at any minute if Simone Reiss weren't there to steel her nerves.

"I'm nervous," Lucille confides. "I'm very nervous."

She has reason to be nervous. She has reached the forty-ninth month of her benefits clock, and she can practically hear it ticking. If the hearing today goes well, she will receive a monthly disability check from the federal government for at least three years and perhaps longer. If not, she and her daughters face destitution in a year.

Lucille's eyes dart around the crowded waiting room as other clients come and go and she clutches her billfold tightly on her lap. Her attorney, Andrew Kline, has spent an hour with her this morning, explaining what will happen at the hearing and reviewing questions the judge is likely to ask. But now she imagines a long and grueling cross-examination by the administrative law judge.

A clerk strolls over and hands Lucille her case file, a binder full of government documents, test results, and summaries of testimony.

"You should probably make sure everything is there for your hearing," he says.

Lucille pages through the documents, a blank look on her face. She can read most of the words, but she cannot comprehend much of the content and she plainly cannot evaluate its importance. After a moment, she hands it across to Reiss, who begins leafing through the pages carefully.

Lucille has reached the third stage of an application for Supplemental Security Income. Her first application, a simple document sent by mail, was rejected, as was her written appeal.

This doesn't surprise Simone Reiss or Andrew Kline. SSI, created by Congress to provide a safety net for disabled, blind, and elderly poor people, grew rapidly in the early 1990s and now ten years later there are signs that enrollment is growing rapidly again. It is now much larger than welfare itself, with some six million recipients and nearly $30 billion a year in outlays.[1] Several times during the 1990s Congress tightened eligibility rules after investigations suggested that families were gaming the system to get their "disabled" children on benefits. Now federal authorities routinely turn down all but the most obvious applicants, and it's not unusual for a client like Lucille to reach this appeals stage.

Reiss has worked meticulously to assemble the documents for Lucille's appeal, but still she and the attorney remain anxious. Lucille sits right at the edge of SSI eligibility. If her IQ were below sixty, she would qualify automatically. Applicants with IQs between sixty and seventy must demonstrate some additional disability that prevents them from holding a job. Lucille has taken two IQ tests, one for a consultant employed by Hired and one for a consultant to the government. One test placed her IQ at sixty-eight and the other placed it at seventy-one. But Kline also has a doctor's report that says that Lucille cannot lift heavy objects, cannot stoop or stand for long periods, and has to rest for two hours every afternoon because of painkillers prescribed for her back injury.

"We'll just answer the judge's questions and do our best," Kline says as they are summoned for Lucille's hearing.

The hearing room resembles a courtroom, but smaller and more spartan. The judge, a slender balding man in a black robe, sits next to a large American flag and behind a tiny bench on a dais at the front. Lucille and Kline take their places at one table. A vocational disability expert, hired by the government as an expert witness, sits across from them at a second table. There is just room at the back for Reiss and one observer to sit on a tiny bench.

The judge can see that Lucille is tense, and after reviewing a few technical rules with Kline, he explains the procedure to her.

"Ma'am, the government has a series of rules to see if you qualify for this particular program. We're here today to decide whether you meet those rules. I want you to know that I'm not here to represent the Social Security Administration. I am a neutral in this proceeding. I'm here to review all the evidence and make a recommendation to the government."

With that he asks all parties to raise their right hands and take a pledge to testify truthfully. Then he begins questioning Lucille.

"Did you graduate from high school?"

"No, sir."

"Have you received any additional education since leaving high school?"

"I'm going for my GED at the Adult Basic Education in Brooklyn Park."

"Tell me your marital status. Are you married, single, divorced?"

"Separated."

"Do you have any minor children?"

"Yes, sir, two, aged twelve and sixteen."

"Is there anyone else in your household who is employed outside the home?"

"No."

"Are you receiving any form of public assistance?"

"MFIP."

"Now, isn't there some sort of time limit on that?"

Reiss interjects: "Yes, your honor, there is a sixty-month limit on MFIP benefits. My client is in her forty-ninth month."

"Do you have a driver's license?"

"No."

"When was the last time you were working?"

"February of last year."

"Where was that?"

"PUR. A company called PUR."

"What was that name again?"

"PUR. They make water filters."

"How long did you work there?"

"Three months."

"What did they have you doing there?"

"Lifting parts and putting them in boxes."

"Did you get that on your own, or did someone help you find that job?"

"I got it on my own."

"Now, this schooling that you're doing now. Is that an everyday thing?"

"It's Monday through Thursday."

"You ride the bus to get there?"

"Yes."

"What are the hours?"

"Nine to one, Monday through Thursday."

"Thank you very much. Now, Mr. Kline. I believe there is some hard evidence, some x-rays, of a problem in your client's back?"

"Yes, Your Honor. The x-ray evidence is Exhibit Two-F, page eleven. Partial sacrilization of the L-five body."

The judge calls Reiss to the witness table.

"Ms. Reiss, I believe you are her employment counselor. What's your understanding of your client's employment limitations?"

"There are limits on the hours she can work before she has to rest."

"I see that. The doctor has put a limitation of twenty hours a week. Why is that?"

"Because of the pain in her back. She has to rest periodically."

Kline adds, "Your Honor, she is on a generic painkiller for her lower-back pain. Some people on this generic need to take naps because it induces drowsiness."

"Ms. Reiss, what is your employment plan for this client?"

"Originally we had her on housing search and Adult Basic Education. That's not actually a GED program. She's not quite ready for the GED program. She wasn't able to handle both of those, so we switched her plan to housing search for the summer."

The judge leafs through Lucille's case file, reviewing the medical evidence. Lucille has been evaluated by two vocational therapists, one employed by Hired and one by the Social Security Administration. Both assessed her ability to lift various weights, to stand for long periods, to bend and carry objects. Hired's expert says that fifteen pounds is the maximum that Lucille can regularly lift.

Kline notes the discrepancy between the two experts and remarks, "I would argue these both indicate severe work-related limitations."

The judge turns to the government's expert witness. "My impression is that these do represent some significant work-related impairments. What is your view?"

"I would agree with that, Your Honor."

"What about the fifteen-pound limitation? The agency's expert seems to think that's a pretty serious limitation."

"I would agree, Your Honor."

The judge reviews a second part of Lucille's vocational evaluation, a checklist of her ability to perform various workplace duties.

"Now, if I had an individual who, out of sixteen work aptitudes, had ten of those aptitudes checked 'poor to none,' would that represent a serious work limitation? I'm looking down this list: 'Ability to handle work-related stress, none. Ability to complete a full work week, poor. Ability to complete a normal work routine without supervision, none. Ability to deal with the public, poor.' Would you disagree that these are serious work limitations?"

"I don't believe so, Your Honor."

"Mr. Kline, it strikes me that the IQ scores I see here are valid, and the level of functionality that I see in your client makes me think that, on balance, the therapist who found a serious work impairment is pretty close to right. Still, there is this divergence between the two vocational experts."

Then, addressing Lucille, he says, "Ma'am, I'm going to make a recommendation in your favor for now, and then put a two-year review on it. I think the evidence before us today shows a serious work limitation.

"But I have to tell you, at age thirty-one, the Social Security Administration is not going to support you for another thirty-five years. This agency has thousands of employees and sooner or later one of them is going to find you ineligible for benefits.

"I'm going to find for you today, but you are too young to

count on this program forever. So I would encourage you to use this time wisely. Get that GED you're trying to get. Get yourself into the workforce. Make the best of this time. OK, that's it. Very best of luck to you."

Lucille, Reiss, and Kline file out of the hearing room, slightly dazed by the speed of the hearing and by the favorable verdict. They reassemble in the waiting room to assess the good news and review what just happened. The slightest hint of a smile plays on Lucille's face, but she is still rocking just perceptibly from residual anxiety. Kline explains that the judge's decision is merely a recommendation, but that it will almost certainly prevail with the Social Security Administration and that Lucille will start receiving checks shortly.

"I'm happy," she says. "I'm very happy. I want to thank that judge."

Lucille already is thinking about ways to use the benefit check: new bunk beds for her daughters, possibly a down payment on a house so she doesn't have to put up with noisy neighbors and apartment living. Still, there is a bittersweet feeling to the verdict. If the disability check comes through, Lucille will leave MFIP and end her relationship with Simone Reiss and Patty Czech, her job counselor on maternity leave. Reiss would like to keep tabs on Lucille and make sure she gets any vocational counseling or social work she needs. But Hennepin County's MFIP budget doesn't permit Hired to continue working with clients who have left welfare. Job counselors are overworked and Reiss will have to turn her attention to other clients.

Lucille, however, is not giving up on her plan. She says she wants to go back to Adult Basic Ed and keep plugging away at her GED.

"That judge only gave me two years. I still want an education."

Patty is cooking supper late one September afternoon and musing about the economy. She's been laid off, not once but twice, since we last spoke, and she is rethinking her circumstances and chopping vegetables when her daughter, Samantha, arrives home from school.

"Ew, I don't like coleslaw," the third-grader says.

"It's not coleslaw," Patty replies.

"I don't like sauerkraut."

"It's not sauerkraut either. You'll live. Now go put your things away and I'll make you a snack."

It seems that the golf-course job didn't work out after all. Patty developed a feud with one of the waitresses, who turned out to be the manager's girlfriend. Soon Patty found she was getting bad shifts and fewer hours. She gave her boss an ultimatum— better hours or she would quit—and she lost. By late July she was behind on her bills and the cell-phone company and cable-television company were threatening to cut her off.

"I know, I know. Cable TV. A cell phone. It sounds pretty luxurious for somebody who's on public assistance. But look, I couldn't afford a full-time nanny while my daughter was home for the summer. She plays with friends or she stays home alone. Cable keeps her in the house, where I know she's safe. It's a lot better than network television, and it's a whole lot cheaper than a baby-sitter."

In early August, after applying for jobs at two warehouses, a law firm, and three Target stores, Patty was getting desperate.

"This economy that's supposed to be recovering? I don't think so. There are two hundred other people applying for every job." She has a point. Even though the national economy has been technically in a recovery for most of the year, Minnesota's job market has remained sluggish all summer. In August she applied at Pro Staff, a temporary employment agency, and got a job at a plastics factory in nearby Anoka. This meant leaving for work before 7:00 A.M. and asking a neighbor to put Samantha on the school bus every morning once the school year started. But it was forty hours a week at $9 per hour, which was a lot of money by Patty's reckoning. Then, in the second week of September, the Anoka company lost a set of customers and laid off all its temporary employees.

Now that she's unemployed again, Patty has put off her wedding plans. She and Don have had their first fight—over money, predictably.

"He came by one night and said, 'What have you been doing all day? There's got to be some sort of job for you out there.'"

Patty had reminded him that she hates sitting around the house, that she hates being without money, that she finds going to work much more fun than staying home and washing laundry, and that the job market has turned tight. She says it wasn't a pretty conversation.

But it's not just the argument. Having resisted marriage for most of her adult life, Patty is not about to rush into it now. She has a mental picture of what wedded life should be: a stable household, no fights over money, both partners carrying their weight, both bringing something to the relationship. In this she mirrors a trend discovered by sociologists during the 1990s. The old stereotype of a woman seeking a breadwinner, if ever it was true, has given way to something more bilateral, an understanding that both spouses bring assets and stability to a marriage. Patty puts it more succinctly:

"I want to have my shit together before I tie the knot."

But her ruptured summer reveals something else important about welfare reform. The lives of poor families seldom have neat story lines or tidy endings. Even in Minnesota, which outperforms most states in leading welfare clients to stable jobs, the path off assistance is slow and bumpy. In 1999, when the state surveyed a sample of employed MFIP recipients, it found that they had made steady gains over the course of twelve months, from roughly twenty hours of work each week to roughly thirty hours a week, but that only about one-third had held the same job for a full year. Nearly one-third had taken most of a year to find work, and another third had found one job, lost it, and then found another. More than four-fifths reported high job satisfaction, but barely half said they saw good chances of career advancement. And while most of the working clients had earned raises of fifty cents to a dollar an hour during their first year working, the typical client was still earning just $8 an hour, a wage that, even with full-time hours, would yield less than $17,000 a year.[2]

Despite the summer's tribulations, Patty is feeling rather plucky this autumn afternoon. She has an interview the next day with Kelly Services, a temporary employment agency that specializes in clerical work. Don says it's time for her to give up bartending. "He doesn't like me at a job where nine out of ten men stare at me when they walk by." And Patty has no interest in another factory job: "I'm too old to stand on concrete all day long." She's resolved to polish up her bookkeeping skills, or at least start with a respectable secretarial job.

Patty's persistence seems to stem partly from her own personality and partly from the rules of MFIP. She says she prefers working outside the house to staying home all day with a laundry machine and soap operas. Then too, when she's unemployed she has to file a lot more paperwork with her Anoka County job counselor. "As long as I'm working thirty hours a week, they stay off my back," she says.

But there are some good things happening in her life too. The county has given her a child-care subsidy as long as she's working or looking for work, and that will pay for Samantha to attend a highly praised after-school program at her grade school. Patty worries that the girl spends too much time at home and, because they have moved twice in three years, isn't making friends at school. The other encouraging item is that Mike, Samantha's father, has steady work and has agreed to the county's child-support payment plan.

"The stinker won't tell me how much I'm going to get every month, but as long as I'm working enough hours I'll get to keep the money from him. That should put me up where I can actually have a nice Christmas this year. Cook a real meal and go see my parents. Not like the last two years—stay home and eat frozen pizza."

In this, Patty reflects yet another truth about welfare reform. Welfare recipients seldom glide straight from assistance to full-time work that, by itself, lifts them into affluence. More typically, it is a matter of patching together income from multiple sources: part-time work, child support from an ex-spouse, a tax credit from the government.

This is the elusive arithmetic that Patty still believes she and Don can put together. "If he and I can pull a few more rabbits out of the hat, things will work out. Ten years from now I'll be looking back on this and pretending it never happened."

Two weeks later, toward the end of September, I catch up with Meg at a coffee shop near the University of Minnesota. She is stifling a yawn and ordering a large cappuccino. Meg needs the caffeine; she's working three part-time jobs and her face is even more drawn than the last time we met. But the cappuccino is also an indulgence and a celebration, for Meg's life is finally starting to match her ambitions. She has a job in a medical lab at the university and has enrolled as a part-time student.

The bank job that she found in midsummer had worked out well. She earned enough money to get ahead on her bills and buy the boys back-to-school clothes. The job reminded her how luxurious it felt to have a steady paycheck, and she finally accepted the advice of her Lifetrack job counselor that full-time schooling was not the right path. The job also restored her self-confidence; she could finally balance work and three children, and her boss seemed to think highly of her work. But when the branch manager offered her a permanent job, she said no. After a month at the bank, she had decided she wasn't ready to give up on her first choice, a career of some sort in medicine.

In mid-August she began scrolling through the Web site of the university's medical school and thinking seriously about going back to school. Her housing situation had stabilized: On August 1 she and the children had left the East Side apartment and moved into a city-subsidized townhouse off Interstate-94, closer to Zachary's school and her mother's house. The neighborhood was safer, the place was bigger, and it was dependable housing for at least a year. After Labor Day, Zachary would be in school all day and her mother would be available to watch the baby and Samuel. Finally, her life seemed calm enough to permit a new challenge. One afternoon she drove over to the university campus and wandered through the hospital and laboratory complex near Stadium Village. On a bulletin board outside one of the labs she saw a notice that made her heart pound: an opening for a part-time lab technician. The next day she called the number and was connected to the lab manager. At first the woman said, no, Meg wasn't qualified. She had no undergraduate training and besides, this was a student position. Meg begged. She said she was planning to enroll at the university, which was true, and would take any courses that might help her with the lab work. She offered to take the job as a temporary assignment and apprentice herself to one of the senior lab techs until she learned the ropes. The lab manager thought it over for a moment and then gave Meg the job.

And so, in the first week of September, Meg was back on campus for her third time as a university student and put in her first day at the lab. The work wasn't glamorous; it wasn't really even medicine. Most of the time she was merely entering data into a computer. And the new routine ran her ragged: She worked in the lab twelve hours a week, went to class another nine hours, worked a data-entry job at home for AT&T on nights and week-ends, and occasionally waitressed at an Indian restaurant in nearby Roseville. But every piece of the crazy schedule felt like a founda-tion stone that was building something that Meg wanted.

She pauses, yawns again, and says she has to pinch herself about the lab job. Because she's working in a university facility, she gets free tuition. In addition, the job pays $18 an hour. Between that and the paycheck from AT&T, she can afford to leave the cash-assistance portion of MFIP and stop the ticking of her benefits clock. The university job pays for her health insur-ance. MFIP will provide transitional health insurance for the boys and the baby and guarantee her a child-care subsidy. She's con-fident that when these benefits run out in a year, she will have more hours, and perhaps a raise, in the lab job.

Meg knows that she's lucky to have made this transition so quickly. It would have been impossible if she didn't already have some college coursework behind her and a mother nearby for baby-sitting and emergencies.

"Grandma gets a little cranky sometimes," Meg says. "We're working her pretty hard. But I told her: Just wait, when I finish college, then I'll take care of you."

A few weeks earlier Meg had cited some advice from her dad, to the effect that it can take six months to climb out of a hole that took one month to dig. I ask her if, after two traumatic years, she feels she's dug her way out.

"Oh no, not yet," she says. "It's more like I'm standing on a ledge, high above the street, looking down. You know, you swing your arms in the air to keep from falling off."

In this Meg is probably right. For though her story seems to have a happy ending after one year, this isn't the last chapter. It's just another month in a story with a long and unpredictable future. The baby could get sick, Anthony could show up again, the job could fizzle, school could prove a bust. Even among parents who make it off welfare, research shows, some 20 percent wind up back on assistance again within two years because of the fragile and volatile nature of their lives.[3]

Regrets?

"You know, my mom asked me that the other day. I was at her house for my birthday. She said, 'You're twenty-nine. You could have had your own medical practice by now. You were going to be a doctor.' I said, 'Yeah, I've got my own child-care practice instead.' But I don't know, you have a lot of big goals when you're eighteen." She sips her coffee.

"Actually, I don't have regrets. When you have kids, they're such a blessing. Just watching them grow up, watching them become who they are. Zachary came in the other day and announced that he doesn't like art, but that he wants to start cooking. All I could say was, 'Oh really.' You never know what they're going to say or who they're going to be next."

This equanimity sounds surprising from someone who once set out to finish medical school by age twenty-five. But like many ambitious parents, Meg seems mellowed a bit by life's surprises, by time spent with her children, by using them as a mirror on her own life.

Some evenings she sits on the couch with Zachary after Samuel and the baby have gone to bed. Apart from her mother, she doesn't have a lot of adult company, and she uses Zachary as a sounding board for her plans and frustrations. He uses her to test out his latest passions. He cuts out pictures of houses he would like to live in and countries he would like to visit. She uses the time to encourage his ambitions, and she makes up little maxims to transmit a mother's hopes. "The more time you spend complaining, the less time you have for work." "If you quit you'll never know what might have been." Or simply, "Never quit, never give up."

She writes these maxims down on scraps of paper and tucks them in his backpack while he sleeps. She looks at them and edits them. And sometimes she repeats them to herself.

CHAPTER 12

Unfinished Business: What the Nation Can Learn from Minnesota's Experiment

In the spring of 2002, as Congress prepared to reauthorize the landmark welfare law it had passed six years earlier, the Senate Finance Committee invited economist Isabel Sawhill to testify about her research on poverty and family formation. The Brookings Institution scholar had finished her prepared remarks when the committee chair, Senator Max Baucus of Montana, asked, "What about this MFIP program people are talking about? Why do we keep hearing so much about Minnesota?"

This was not an isolated incident. Ten years after its creation, the Minnesota Family Investment Program had developed a national reputation among poverty experts and it turned up often in conversations about the next phase of welfare reform. President Bill Clinton had cited MFIP's unusual impacts on families and young children during formal remarks on welfare in the spring of 2000, and his administration had awarded Minnesota a high-performance bonus for job placement and job retention that same year. Joel Kvamme and Chuck Johnson from the Minnesota Department of Human Services had been invited to speak at national welfare conferences, and the evaluation team from the Manpower Demonstration Research Corporation was in regular demand on the scholarly conference circuit. Rebecca Blank at the University of Michigan and David Card at the University of California at Berkeley, prominent scholars in the field of employment and poverty, had published a paper arguing that programs like Minnesota's, by combining financial incentives with work requirements, had opened a new conversation among economists about the promise of promoting work while reducing poverty.[1]

The interest in Minnesota's results is not hard to explain, for six years after the passage of the Personal Responsibility and Work Opportunity Act, the welfare revolution of the 1990s remained incomplete.

As an experiment in promoting work, the new federal law had exceeded all expectations. Poor single mothers, the demographic group targeted in welfare reform, had poured into the job market in numbers that economists considered all but unprecedented.[2] The number of families on cash assistance had dropped by an astonishing 50 percent between 1996 and 2001, from 4.4 million to 2.2 million, and the share of Americans on welfare had fallen to the lowest point since 1964.[3] And while the robust job market of the 1990s explained part of this trend, careful studies by economists concluded that changes in the law and government incentives accounted for much of the trend.

From the perspective of poor families, however, the revolution was not quite so promising. Remarkably, there was no comprehensive federal effort to study what became of families who left welfare, or "leavers." But representative studies carried out in several states and by the Urban Institute in Washington, D.C., found that about 20 percent of welfare leavers were back on assistance within two years, and among those who stayed off welfare, about 30 percent never found work.[4] Although these families became largely invisible to the general public, when surveyed they reported substantial material hardships, including shortages of food and a struggle to pay rent and basic bills.[5]

Even the leavers with steady employment found that higher earnings scarcely offset the loss of government benefits, meaning that on average their overall incomes rose hardly at all. Welfare leavers who did find work were earning an average of $700 to $900 per month in the first months after leaving assistance, so that, even including government benefits such as food stamps and the Earned Income Tax Credit, perhaps half of them found that their incomes had gone down, not up, after 1996.[6]

Nor did welfare reform save the taxpayer substantial sums of money, at least not in the first six years. As a technical matter, this was because Congress in 1996 gave states fixed annual block grants with a funding stream that held steady even as welfare caseloads fell. But it was also because states discovered, as many scholars had predicted, that welfare reform was expensive. Governors found that they quickly spent their federal grants on child care, health insurance, and other services that moved needy families into the workplace and helped them stay there. In fiscal year 2001 states actually overspent their federal block grants, drawing down reserves from previous years, with a large share of the money going into work-support services such as child-care subsidies and wage supplements.[7]

Of course, a reduction in welfare dependency on this scale was in itself a huge achievement. It assuaged the public's suspicion that unscrupulous families were cheating the system to stay on welfare, and it rebuilt the nation's confidence in antipoverty programs. It delivered a new message of responsibility to adults on welfare, and many welfare clients interviewed for this book said they appreciated the system's new tools and high expectations. And that the nation could cut its welfare rolls by half without producing a surge in poverty—the nation's poverty rate actually fell throughout the late 1990s—astonished many experts.

Nevertheless, reducing dependency must be considered only a partial and proximate achievement of the welfare revolution. Even the most ardent advocates of welfare reform always claimed that they were seeking some higher goal: not merely to reduce the use of government aid, but to introduce poor families to a better life and a brighter future. This was, after all, the motivating impulse behind public welfare from its earliest days in American history. And even during the Calvinist 1990s, all but the most hardened ideologues agreed that reducing penury was the ultimate aim. "The answer to welfare reform very clearly is to get people out of poverty," said Representative Clay Shaw, a Florida Republican who helped write the Personal Responsibility Act, during the reform debate. "We are at last going to be measured by the number of people we get out of poverty, not the number of people that we pay while they are in poverty."[8]

Six years after Congress passed the Personal Responsibility Act, it was not clear that the law had achieved this larger goal. The single broadest piece of evidence cited by the law's defenders is that the nation's poverty rates fell sharply after 1996, a period when thousands of families left assistance. But Wendell Primus at the Center on Budget and Policy Priorities has documented that poverty was falling faster *before* 1996 than afterward, which suggests it was a booming economy, not a change in the law, that raised the incomes of poor families. Significantly, the nation's poverty rate began inching up again in 2001, the moment that the red-hot economy began to cool.

As for the well-being of poor children, a steady stream of studies suggested that welfare reform had produced little or no improvement. In 2002 Kristin Moore, the respected head of Child Trends in Washington, D.C., surveyed a broad range of social indicators, such as reading scores and health statistics, and about the best she could conclude was that the overhaul of welfare had done no harm. "Overall, we can see dramatic changes in the lives of parents as a result of welfare reform, but little change in child outcomes," Moore wrote. "We have looked at dozens of indicators, and they show neither a pattern of solid improvement nor substantial decline. Low-income children—including children touched by welfare reform—continue to lag far behind all other children on these measures, with little evidence that they are beginning to catch up."[9]

How could such a dramatic transformation in the work behavior of poor parents produce so little progress for their families? Isabel Sawhill spoke for many of her colleagues in the research community when she observed that welfare reform, so far, consisted of the stick more than the carrot. That is, it had pushed thousands of families into the workforce without saying much about what would happen to them once they got there. It was true that since the mid-1980s the federal government had adopted several measures to reward work. In 1993, at the urging of President Clinton, Congress had enacted a large expansion of the Earned Income Tax Credit, which used the federal income-tax system to pay cash credits to low-income workers. By 2001, the tax credit actually paid more money to poor families than the cash welfare system. In 1996 Congress had approved a big increase in federal child-care subsidies, and in 1997 it enacted an expansion of the Medicaid program aimed at helping the working poor. But even so, the ideal of "make work pay" remained more theory than reality. The share of eligible families who actually received food stamps and Medicaid was going down, not up.[10] And even after including food stamps and the tax credit, as many as half of the families who left welfare remained stuck in poverty.[11]

In Minnesota, the results were different. They were certainly imperfect, for perhaps one-third of Minnesota Family Investment Program recipients remained unemployed even after two or three years in the system, and a large share of MFIP alumni were still struggling along in jobs that left them at or near the poverty line. But as state and federal researchers would document by 2002, Minnesota far exceeded other states at lifting welfare families out of poverty, placed most welfare recipients in above-poverty level jobs, and outperformed the national averages in extending health insurance and child-care subsidies to the working poor. In other words, it delivered on the twin goals of raising employment and reducing poverty.

Despite its success on these measures, and despite its growing reputation, MFIP remained subject to two criticisms. The first was that, by paying partial benefits to recipients even after they found work, it actually extended the dependency of poor families, rather than reducing it. The second was that MFIP embedded attractive benefits such as child-care subsidies and wage supplements within the welfare system, rather than making them broadly available to the working poor. Many scholars, on the political left and right, felt that states should divorce these benefits from the welfare system and move to a "seamless" system in which poor adults could receive such work supports, whether or not they applied for cash welfare.

As an empirical matter, the dependency critique is not quite correct. It's true that MFIP recipients with jobs were more likely to be drawing some small benefit from the state than their predecessors in AFDC. But one of the most powerful findings from the county field trials was that MFIP clients were less likely to rely on welfare alone, compared with the AFDC group, precisely because they increased their work and earnings so substantially.[12] Subsequent findings from the statewide version of MFIP—that some 70 percent of new applicants left welfare within two years—

also suggested that the system was doing more to reduce dependency than to sustain it.

There is also a philosophical side to the dependency argument. To some social conservatives, even a single dollar of government benefits is a signal of dependency, and the government's aim should be to wean poor families from all support. But this seems an extreme definition of "dependent." Surely a poor single mother who makes the effort to find a job, arrange child care, and then work thirty to forty hours a week while raising small children is demonstrating the virtues of enterprise and responsibility as most Americans would define them. The danger is not that she will find herself addicted to some modest government benefit, but that, having made this strenuous effort, she will find that her family remains mired in struggle and hardship because the government has ruled her ineligible for aid.

The seamlessness critique is harder to answer, for in an ideal world the government might guarantee health insurance, high-quality child care, and a living wage for all working parents. But it's worth remembering that the impulse for welfare reform had its roots in a perception that the welfare system was broken, not in a crusade to make life better for the working poor. Building work incentives into the welfare system was a natural, and now proven, tool to ease recipients into the job market.

If the creators of MFIP hadn't solved all of these puzzles, they had met or exceeded their original goals and, in addition, had shed new light on a dilemma that had long vexed policy makers and welfare scholars. On the one hand, researchers had known for some time that financial incentives alone were unlikely to produce large increases in work effort by poor adults. Evaluations of a negative income tax in the 1970s, known as the Seattle/Denver Income Maintenance Experiments, together with periodic testing of earnings disregards in AFDC after 1967, had produced discouraging results with respect to promoting work. On the other hand, researchers had learned that simply imposing work requirements did little to lift families out of poverty. In the late 1990s, the Manpower Demonstration Research Corporation and the U.S. Department of Health and Human Services had begun publishing a sweeping review of evaluations of various welfare-to-work experiments conducted by the states between the late 1980s and the mid-1990s. Their report, known as the National Evaluation of Welfare-to-Work Strategies, concluded that rigorous work requirements could encourage welfare recipients to work more and earn more money, but that these programs ultimately had little impact on poverty because the client families lost a dollar of benefits for every dollar of earned income.[13]

But there was a third set of experiments under the MDRC microscope. These included MFIP; an initiative known as the New Hope Project in Milwaukee, Wisconsin; and a program called the Self-Sufficiency Project in two provinces in Canada. These programs varied in their tactics and their target populations, but they had one thing in common: all three employed a combination of employment mandates and financial incentives. In other words, they required work and they rewarded it. And these programs suggested that, if the government deployed a combination of work requirements and work incentives properly, it could achieve the twin goals of employment and poverty reduction. Summarizing the findings, MDRC's Gordon Berlin wrote that the three experiments "provide encouraging evidence that making work pay (in conjunction with other services and conditions) can both increase work and reduce poverty among welfare recipients without reducing employment rates among the working poor."[14]

Isabel Sawhill had studied these findings, and she took the research a step further. In an essay published in the spring of 2001 she argued that if the government expanded tax credits for the working poor, raised the minimum wage, and increased child-care subsidies to poor families—but then required the recipient parents to work something like thirty hours a week—it could produce a huge reduction in the nation's poverty rate. Evaluating these proposals with an economist's precision, she predicted that for every $1 the government spent on such a strategy, it could raise the incomes of target families by more than $1.50. In other words, this blend of tactics could convert the notorious "leaky bucket" of antipoverty policy into one that overflowed.[15]

But the make-work-pay research didn't stop with financial results. The evaluators at MDRC had designed the evaluations of MFIP, New Hope, and Project Self-Sufficiency so that they could examine impacts on marriage rates and child well-being, and so that they could isolate which effects were due to higher income and which were due to work alone. Here again, their findings were dramatic. "A key finding from the experiments is that impacts on child achievement and behavior were consistently more positive in programs that provided financial and in-kind supports (earnings supplements) for work than those that did not," wrote Pamela Morris of MDRC and Greg Duncan of Northwestern University. "These findings suggest that policymakers face a choice when deciding which welfare reforms are best for children. They can increase parental self-sufficiency, provide few benefits to children, and save government money. Or they can increase parental employment, raise family income, provide benefits to children, and increase government spending with earnings supplement programs."[16] These findings were reinforced in 2003, when MDRC released a follow-up study on the New Hope Project, showing that its impacts on family income and child well-being were remarkably resilient and actually continued for at least two years after the recipient families had left the subsidy program.

This sort of research made MFIP and its peers famous in the research community and inspired hope among advocates for the poor. Yet it must be said that even in Minnesota the novel approach to welfare never quite escaped its own set of political constraints—the constraints of a federalist system that penalizes any state that deviates too far from the national norm. The version of MFIP that operated in county field trials from 1994 to 1997 may have been the most generous welfare-to-work program attempted by any state during the 1990s, both in the size of its cash benefits and the flexibility of its work rules, and many Minnesota legislators could never accommodate themselves to this degree of generosity, whatever the program's empirical successes. This tension dominated legislative debate in 1997, when lawmakers trimmed MFIP's benefits in the process of adapting it for statewide use, and it lingered in the background in 2001, when the legislature had to decide how Minnesota would treat welfare recipients reaching their federal time limits.

In short, Minnesota's technical achievement—designing a welfare system that promoted work while reducing poverty—was unambiguous. But its political achievement—building political consensus around a progressive version of welfare reform— seemed to ebb and flow. In years of budget surplus, the legislature honored the state's commitment to reducing poverty, funding intensive services for the most disadvantaged families and adopting generous extension rules for recipients reaching federal time limits. But in lean years, the opposite occurred. In 2003, for example, when Minnesota faced its worst budget deficit in a generation, the legislature adopted a set of recommendations by Governor Tim Pawlenty that reduced MFIP's cash benefits for most families, established tougher new application procedures, and increased the penalties that counties could impose on noncompliant families. The result was to reduce both MFIP's simplicity and its antipoverty impact. Of course, much the same pattern emerged at the federal level. In the late 1990s, under President Clinton, Congress created new programs to supplement welfare-to-work funding and to subsidize health insurance for children of the working poor. By 2002, President George W. Bush and his allies in Congress accused states of going soft on the 1996 welfare work requirements and insisted that work, and work alone, was the best path out of poverty.

To Joel Kvamme, who had retired from government service by this time, it was as if the nation's leaders had chosen to ignore a decade of careful research and practical experience, to pretend that the nation had not just conducted an extraordinary six-year experiment in welfare reform. It was as if they could not relinquish the popular but misleading stereotypes that had dominated welfare politics twenty years earlier and launched his own long inquiry into welfare dynamics.

Because those stereotypes triggered the modern period of welfare reform and proved so tenacious as it unfolded, in closing it's worth considering them again. One of these views held that the welfare poor somehow stood outside of society's mainstream, that they had never grasped the American ideals of self-discipline and pride, that they lived within a self-contained subculture of sloth and destructive behavior. This view was implicit in a growing literature on the "culture of poverty" and it was explicit in the language of President Ronald Reagan. "We're in danger of creating a permanent culture of poverty as inescapable as any chain or bond," Reagan said in a radio address in February 1986. "A second and separate America, an America of lost dreams and stunted lives."[17]

A second view, quite different from the first but advanced by many of the same social conservatives, held that the welfare poor were just like other Americans, except for lack of a job. In this view, if the government could push welfare recipients into the labor market, it could count on the rigors of work to instill the admirable personal virtues and lift poor families into the social and economic mainstream. This view was implicit in the Personal Responsibility Act, since it ended cash assistance for most families after five years, and it was explicit in some of the remarks made by its supporters. "Study after study has now shown that work is the best way to reduce poverty," Representative Wally Herger of California argued during debate over reauthorization of the 1996 law.[18]

From the stories of the three women in this book, it should be plain that neither of these conceptions quite captures the reality of life on welfare. Patty, Meg, and Lucille do not stand outside the American mainstream. All three have worked, two have been married, one aspires to graduate from college. All three live in mixed-race working-class neighborhoods where they struggle, more or less capably, to raise their children in safety and self-respect. They have certainly made poor choices and irresponsible decisions, but that is quite different from saying that they reject society's consensus definitions of success and propriety.

But it would be equally wrong to say that unemployment—and perhaps the lack of a spouse—is the only barrier standing between these women and economic security. It is certainly true, as the authors of the Personal Responsibility Act argued, that these women would be better off with good jobs and responsible partners. But to that list of missing assets one could easily add physical health, intellectual acuity, reliable relatives, stable housing, trustworthy friends, safe neighborhoods, and dependable transportation. In short, each of these women, like thousands of others on public assistance, needed a social partner as well as a job.

This was exactly the insight that struck the people who created MFIP. They spurned the simple political formulations of the time, because they knew that the lives of poor people are complicated. They imposed new expectations on the families who sought government assistance because they knew that the American public expected it. But they offered these struggling parents a form of partnership because they believed that this might lead to better lives for the nation's poor. And, whether or not the nation ultimately listened, they were right.

Notes

Introduction

1. See, for example, Alicia H. Munnell, ed., *Lessons from the Income Maintenance Experiments* (Boston: Federal Reserve Bank of Boston, 1987), pp. 3–21.

2. Cited in Ron Haskins, "The Second Most Important Issue," paper presented at The New World of Welfare, Washington, D.C., February 2001, p. 2.

3. Michael B. Katz, *In the Shadow of the Poorhouse* (New York: Basic Books, 1996), p. 17.

4. *New York Times*, July 27, 1990, p. 1.

5. *The Brookings Review*, Summer 2001, p. 43.

6. Katz, p. 326.

7. Manpower Demonstration Research Corporation, Final Report on the Minnesota Family Investment Program, Summary, May 2000.

8. Ron Haskins, "Effects of Welfare Reform at Three Years," paper presented at Understanding Poverty in America, Institute for Research on Poverty, Madison, Wisconsin, May 2000, pp. 2–6.

9. John Karl Scholz and Kara Levine, "The Evolution of Income Support Policy," paper presented at Understanding Poverty in America, Madison, Wisconsin, May 2000, p. 44 and appendix tables.

1. Welfare 101

1. *Indicators of Welfare Dependence, Annual Report to Congress, 2001* (Washington, D.C.: U.S. Department of Health and Human Services), p. A-14.

2. Reality Check

1. Department of Human Services spreadsheet, May 1986, archives of Randy Johnson.

2. Author interview, December 2001.

3. *Star Tribune*, February 23, 1986, p. 9B.

4. *Star Tribune*, March 19, 1986, p. 1A.

5. Author interviews, November and December 2001. The full commission roster was as follows. Republican nominees: Randy Johnson, Hennepin County commissioner; Norbert Bruegmann, director, Jackson County Human Services; Pege Jennings, social worker, Steele County Social Services; Jack Jones, child protection worker, Ramsey County Human Services; Dr. Bruce Wolff, surgeon, Mayo Clinic, Rochester, Minnesota. Democratic nominees: Monsignor J. Jerome Boxleitner, director, Catholic Charities of Minnesota; Mark Andrew, Hennepin County commissioner; Pat Fredley, director, New Directions for Displaced Homemakers, Detroit Lakes, Minnesota; Luanne Nyberg, director, Children's Defense Fund of Minnesota; Annie Young, coordinator, Project Self-Sufficiency, Minneapolis.

6. Commission minutes, Welfare Reform Commission archives of Randy Johnson.

7. *Population Notes*, September 1984 (St. Paul: Minnesota State Planning Agency, Office of the State Demographer). Several national studies had also examined the question of welfare migration. Although their findings differed, most concluded that the share of poor families who move from one state to another in any year is extremely small and that net national migration from low-benefit states to high-benefit states is small or nonexistent. See, for example, Russell L. Hanson and John T. Hartman, "Do Welfare Magnets Attract?" February 1994, Institute for Research on Poverty, University of Wisconsin.

8. Office of Jobs Policy memorandum, July 16, 1986, archives of the Minnesota Historical Society.

9. Joel Kvamme, "Use of AFDC by Single Parents," unpublished statistical memorandum (St. Paul: Minnesota Department of Human Services, March 1985), p. 16.

10. Ibid., p. 6.

11. Ibid., p. 1.

12. Joel Kvamme, "Utilization of AFDC in Minnesota," unpublished statistical memorandum (St. Paul: Minnesota Department of Human Services, July 1986), p. 21.

13. Ibid., p. 11.

14. Ibid., p. 12.

15. *Welfare Reform in Minnesota: Successes and Challenges for MFIP Families* (St. Paul: Minnesota Department of Human Services, December 2000), p. 4.

16. *Star Tribune*, April 16, 1986, p. 1B.

17. Author interviews, December 2001.

18. Testimony of Barbara Kaufman, archives of Randy Johnson.

19. Written testimony submitted by witnesses, archives of Randy Johnson.

20. Author interviews and unpublished memorandum of Luanne Nyberg and Pege Jennings.

21. *St. Paul Pioneer Press-Dispatch*, October 30, 1986.

22. *Report of the Minnesota Commission on Welfare Reform*, December 1, 1986.

3. Real Life, Fall 2001

1. *Welfare Reform in Minnesota: Successes and Challenges for MFIP Families* (St. Paul: Minnesota Department of Human Services, December 2000), table 6.2.

2. Brooklyn Park Police Department dispatch logs.

3. *Welfare Reform in Minnesota: Successes and Challenges for MFIP Families* (St. Paul: Minnesota Department of Human Services, December

2000), table 6.6, and *Population Notes*, Minnesota State Planning Agency, May 2001, p. 3.

4. Briefing document by Chuck Johnson, "The Minnesota Family Investment Program at Five Years," Minnesota Department of Human Services, September 2002.

4. Remaking Welfare

1. The state later discovered that the PATHS acronym already was being used in the private sector and renamed the welfare-to-work program STRIDE.

2. Office of Jobs Policy office memorandum, September 25, 1987, Minnesota Historical Society.

3. The Minnesota Family Investment Plan, "Data Digest" (St. Paul: Minnesota Department of Human Services, December 1988), p. 4.

4. Ibid., p. 6.

5. Unpublished memo to Sandra Gardebring and Charles Schultz, February 1987.

6. Federal Application to Implement the Minnesota Family Investment Plan (St. Paul: Minnesota Department of Human Services, September 1990), section IV, p. 3.

7. Ibid., section IV, p. 6.

8. *Star Tribune*, March 8, 1989, p. 1B.

9. Author interviews.

10. Author interviews.

11. The seven counties where MFIP underwent field trials were Anoka, Hennepin, Dakota, Mille Lacs, Morrison, Sherburne, and Todd. Ramsey County joined the field trials later.

5. Real Life, Winter 2001–2002

1. The most comprehensive of these studies was the National Evaluation of Welfare-to-Work Strategies, funded by the U.S. Department of Health and Human Services and conducted by the Manpower Demonstration Research Corporation with other research organizations. NEWWS studied eleven welfare-to-work programs conducted in

seven states between 1988 and 1996. It compared work-first strategies and education-and-training strategies, and evaluated both against control groups of recipients in traditional AFDC. In the final NEWWS report, the evaluators concluded that all eleven welfare-to-work programs out-performed AFDC at moving recipients into jobs, raising their earnings, and reducing their use of welfare. In a much-cited result, they also found that the work-first programs increased employment and earnings more than education programs in the first two to three years of a recipient's participation, and that the education strategies had "disappointing" results in raising long-term earnings of recipients in ways that might compensate for their time spent in school. They also found that work-first programs were much cheaper for taxpayers than education pro-grams, so that the overall benefit-cost ratio for work-first programs greatly exceeded that of education programs. But the evaluators also found that graduates of work-first programs achieved little long-term growth in earnings, so that by the end of five years their earnings advan-tage had faded relative to earnings of graduates of education-oriented programs. The evaluators also found no significant gain in the overall incomes of the recipient families, because gains in earned income were offset by loss of government benefits. In another much-cited result, they found that by far the most powerful of the eleven programs was one oper-ated in Portland, Oregon, which used a "mixed strategy": it encouraged recipients to find work quickly, but it also encouraged them to choose good jobs with relatively high wages, and then to combine part-time training with employment. Source: Gayle Hamilton, *Moving People from Welfare to Work, Lessons from the National Evaluation of Welfare-to-Work Strategies* (Washington, D.C.: U.S. Department of Health and Human Services, July 2002).

2. Elaine Sorensen and Helen Oliver, "Child Support Reforms in PRWORA: Initial Impacts" (Washington, D.C.: The Urban Institute, 2002), table 2.

3. Ibid., p. 9.

4. Ibid., p. 10.

5. Irwin Garfinkel, "Child Support in the New World of Welfare,"

in Rebecca Blank and Ron Haskins, ed., *The New World of Welfare* (Washington, D.C.: The Brookings Institution, 2001), p. 450.

6. Ibid., p. 445.

6. A New Federal Challenge

1. Manpower Demonstration Research Corporation, "Preliminary Findings for Single Parents in MFIP," January 1997.

2. Pamela A. Holcomb et al., *Income Support and Social Services for Low-Income People in Florida* (Washington, D.C.: The Urban Institute, February 1999).

3. Kristin S. Seefeldt et al., *Income Support and Social Services for Low-Income People in Michigan* (Washington, D.C.: The Urban Institute, July 1998).

4. *State Welfare Waivers: An Overview* (Washington, D.C.: U.S. Department of Health and Human Services, June 1997), tables I.A and II.B.

5. Gretchen G. Kirby et al., *Income Support and Social Services for Low-Income People in Massachusetts* (Washington, D.C.: The Urban Institute, December 1997).

6. *State Welfare Waivers: An Overview.*

7. Kristin S. Seefeldt et al., *Income Support and Social Services for Low-Income People in Wisconsin* (Washington, D.C.: The Urban Institute, December 1998), p. 30.

8. Susan Gooden et al., "Matching Applicants with Services: Initial Assessments in the Milwaukee County W-2 Program" (New York: Manpower Demonstration Research Corporation, November 2001), page iii.

9. Author interviews, January 2002.

10. Author interviews, January 2002.

11. Author interviews. The task force's full membership was: Senators Linda Berglin (D), Sheila Kiscaden (R), Pat Piper (D), Martha Robertson (R), Don Samuelson (D), and Dan Stevens (R); and Representatives Lynda Boudreau (R), Fran Bradley (R), Kevin Goodno (R), Lee Greenfield (D), Loren Jennings (D), and Linda Wejcman (D), with Democratic representative Tom Huntley also participating occasionally.

12. Author interviews.

13. Author interviews and unpublished minutes from the Minnesota Department of Human Services.

14. Author interviews and Department of Human Services minutes.

15. Welfare Reform Work Group, Status Summary, February 18, 1997, unpublished Department of Human Services memorandum.

16. *Star Tribune*, January 22, 1997, p. A12.

17. Author interviews.

18. For several subsequent years, members of the legislature found the money to avoid imposing this offset for housing subsidies.

19. Minnesota House of Representatives, *Session Weekly*, May 23, 1997.

20. Author interview.

21. Author interview.

22. Sheila Rafferty Zedlewski in *The Future of Children: Children and Welfare Reform* (Los Altos, California: The David and Lucile Packard Foundation, Spring 2002).

23. Ibid.

24. Kathryn Tout et al., *Recent Changes in Minnesota Welfare and Work, Child Care and Child Welfare Systems* (Washington, D.C.: The Urban Institute, June 2001).

25. *Kids Count Data Book* (Baltimore: Annie E. Casey Foundation, 2002), p. 105.

26. Gayle Hamilton et al., *National Evaluation of Welfare-to-Work Strategies: How Effective Are Different Welfare-to-Work Approaches?* (Washington, D.C.: U.S. Department of Health and Human Services, Administration for Children and Families, Office of Planning and Evaluation, November 2001), Executive Summary.

27. *MFIP Monthly Report*, Minnesota Department of Human Services, September 1998.

7. Real Life, Spring 2002

1. "Affordable Rental Housing at Risk" (Minneapolis: Family Housing Fund of Minnesota, July 1998), p. 2.

2. Stephen Zuckerman et al., *Health Insurance, Access, and Health Status of Nonelderly Adults* (Washington, D.C.: The Urban Institute, 2001), p. 2.

3. *The State of Children in America's Union* (Washington, D.C.: The Children's Defense Fund, 2002), p. 4.

4. *Welfare Reform in Minnesota: Successes and Challenges for MFIP Families* (St. Paul: Minnesota Department of Human Services, December 2000), appendix 9.

5. Dan Bloom and Don Winstead, "Sanctions and Welfare Reform" (Washington, D.C.: The Brookings Institution, 2002), p. 4.

6. Bloom and Winstead, p. 3. Also Minnesota Department of Human Services, unpublished interoffice memo, March 1996.

7. Russell Overby, "Summary of Survey of Welfare Recipients Employed or Sanctioned for Noncompliance" (Memphis: University of Tennessee, 1997), and unpublished data, Minnesota Department of Human Services.

8. Bruce Fuller et al., "Welfare Reform and Child Care Options for Low-Income Families," in *Children and Welfare Reform* (Los Altos, Calif.: The David and Lucile Packard Foundation, Spring 2002).

9. Lisa Gennetian and Cynthia Miller, "Reforming Welfare and Rewarding Work, Final Report on the Minnesota Family Investment Program, volume 2" (New York: Manpower Demonstration Research Corporation, September 2000).

8. Making Welfare Work

1. Greg Owen, Ellen Shelton, and Corinna Roy, "Filling the Gaps in Welfare Reform, Final Report to the McKnight Foundation" (St. Paul: Wilder Research Center, August 2000), pp. 42 and 53.

2. Greg Owen et al., *Whose Job Is It? Employers' Views on Welfare Reform* (St. Paul: Wilder Research Center, May 2000), pp. 15–20.

3. Owen, Shelton, and Roy, p. 40.

4. Minnesota Department of Human Services, October 2001 TANF Fact Sheet.

5. Owen, Shelton, and Roy, p. 11.

6. Virginia Knox, Cynthia Miller, and Lisa A. Gennetian, *Reforming Welfare and Rewarding Work: Summary of the Final Report on the Minnesota Family Investment Program* (New York: Manpower Demonstration Research Corporation, May 2000), p. 11.

7. Ibid., p. 19.

8. Ibid., p. 21.

9. Ibid., pp. 11 and 20.

10. Ibid., pp. 11 and 20.

11. Ibid., pp. 13–15.

12. "The Minnesota Family Investment Program: A Comprehensive Welfare Reform Plan," unpublished memorandum, Minnesota Department of Human Services, February 1991.

13. *Minnesota Family Investment Program Longitudinal Study: One Year After Baseline* (St. Paul: Minnesota Department of Human Services, December 2000), p. ii.

14. U.S. Department of Health and Human Services, Administration for Children and Families Web site, www.acf.dhhs.gov/news/stats.

15. Author's calculations from Minnesota Department of Human Services administrative data.

16. *Welfare Reform in Minnesota: Successes and Challenges for MFIP Families* (St. Paul: Minnesota Department of Human Services), p. 9.

17. Ibid., p. 12.

18. Author's calculations from Minnesota Department of Human Services administrative data.

19. "Welfare Reform: Select Client Outcomes in Urban Minnesota and Wisconsin," unpublished memo, Minnesota Department of Human Services, March 2000.

20. *Economic Status of Welfare Recipients* (St. Paul: Office of the Minnesota Legislative Auditor, January 2002), p. 44.

9. Real Life, Summer 2002

1. Mary Jo Bane and David Ellwood, *Welfare Realities: From Rhetoric to Reform* (Cambridge, Mass.: Harvard University Press, 1994), p. 57.

10. The Limits of Welfare Reform

1. Sandra Danziger, Mary Corcoran, et al., "Barriers to the Employment of Welfare Recipients" (Ann Arbor: University of Michigan Poverty Research and Training Center, February 2000), pp. 9–10.

2. Ibid., p. 11.

3. *Welfare Reform: Moving Hard-to-Employ Recipients into the Workforce* (Washington, D.C.: General Accounting Office, March 2001).

4. Ibid., p. 6. The studied states were California, Connecticut, Florida, Maryland, Michigan, and Washington.

5. Sheila Zedlewski and Pamela Loprest, *How Well Does TANF Fit the Needs of the Most Disadvantaged Families?* (Washington, D.C.: The Urban Institute, December 2000), p. 22.

6. Author interview, April 2002.

7. Unpublished administrative data, Minnesota Department of Human Services, August 2, 2002.

11. Real Life, Fall 2002

1. *Annual Report of the Supplemental Security Income Program* (Washington, D.C.: U.S. Social Security Administration, May 2000), p. 34.

2. *Minnesota Family Investment Program Longitudinal Study: One Year after Baseline* (St. Paul: Minnesota Department of Human Services, December 2000), pp. 59, 64, and 75.

3. Pamela Loprest, "Who Returns to Welfare?" (Washington, D.C.: The Urban Institute, September 2002), p. 1.

12. Unfinished Business

1. Rebecca M. Blank and David E. Card, ed., *Finding Jobs: Work and Welfare Reform* (New York: Russell Sage Foundation, 2000), p. 13.

2. Robert A. Moffitt, "From Welfare to Work: What the Evidence Shows" (Washington, D.C.: The Brookings Institution, January 2002), p. 1.

3. U.S. Department of Health and Human Services, Administration for Children and Families Web site, www.acf.dhhs.gov/news/stats.

4. Pamela Loprest, "Making the Transition from Welfare to

Work," in Alan Weil and Kenneth Finegold, ed., *Welfare Reform: The Next Act* (Washington, D.C.: The Urban Institute Press, 2002), pp. 19 and 21.

5. Pamela Loprest, *How Are Families That Left Welfare Doing?* (Washington, D.C.: The Urban Institute, April 2001), p. 6.

6. Ron Haskins, Isabel Sawhill, and Kent Weaver, "Welfare Reform: An Overview of Effects to Date" (Washington, D.C.: The Brookings Institution, January 2001), pp. 6–7.

7. Sharon Parrott and Zoe Neuberger, *States Need More Federal TANF Funds* (Washington, D.C.: Center on Budget and Policy Priorities, May 2002).

8. Congressional Record, House of Representatives, July 24, 1996.

9. Kristin Anderson Moore and Martha J. Zaslow, *The Unfinished Business of Welfare Reform* (Washington, D.C.: Child Trends, April 2002), p. 10.

10. Robert Greenstein and Jocelyn Guyer, "Supporting Work through Medicaid and Food Stamps," in Rebecca Blank and Ron Haskins, ed., *The New World of Welfare* (Washington, D.C.: The Brookings Institution, 2001), pp. 335–47.

11. Loprest, p. 5.

12. Cynthia Miller et al., *Reforming Welfare and Rewarding Work: Final Report on the Minnesota Family Investment Program* (New York: Manpower Demonstration Research Corporation, September 2000), table 4.2.

13. Gayle Hamilton, *Moving People from Welfare to Work: Lessons from the National Evaluation of Welfare-to-Work Strategies* (Washington, D.C.: U.S. Department of Health and Human Services, July 2002), chapter 4.

14. Gordon Berlin, *Encouraging Work and Reducing Poverty: The Impact of Work Incentive Programs* (New York: Manpower Demonstration Research Corporation, 2000), p. 43.

15. Isabel Sawhill and Adam Thomas, *A Hand Up for the Bottom Third: Toward a New Agenda for Low-Income Working Families* (Washington, D.C.: The Brookings Institution, May 2001), p. 3.

16. Pamela A. Morris and Greg J. Duncan, "Which Welfare Reforms Are Best for Children?" (Washington, D.C.: The Brookings Institution, September 2001), p. 6.

17. *Star Tribune*, February 16, 1986, p. 27A.

18. Author interview, August 2002.

Index

Aaron, Henry, 127

Activism, 14, *See also* Protests and protesting

AFDC. *See* Aid to Families with Dependent Children (AFDC)

African Americans: as welfare recipients, 2, 41

Aid to Families with Dependent Children (AFDC): abolished, 4; attacks on, 12–14, 16, 30; bureaucracy of, 30; as catchall system, 58; compared to MFIP, 65, 93, 125–27, 190; as complicated and punitive, 27–28; conversion to MFIP, 87–88, 89–90; cuts and reductions, 12–13; dissatisfaction with, xviii, 25; diversion strategy, 90; duration of recipients' use, 22; as entitlement system, 4; as federalist hybrid, 11–12; and inflation,

53; as institutional trap, 63; invisible clients, 151–52; lack of initiatives, 26; narrower benefits vs. MFIP, 93; studies of, 202–3n1; total annual income of recipients, 57; and welfare reform, 11–31, 47–65

Ames, Libby, 77–78

Andrew, Mark, xix, 200n5

ANF. *See* Assessing the New Federalism (ANF)

Annie E. Casey Foundation, 100

Anoka County (Minnesota), viii, 7, 74, 202n11

Antipoverty activism, 14. *See also* Protests and protesting

Antipoverty policy, xvi–xvii; confidence in, 187; federal regulation, 49; "leaky bucket" of, 193

Assessing the New Federalism (ANF): research project, viii

Dave Hage is a journalist specializing in labor, economics, and poverty. As an editorial writer at the Minneapolis-based *Star Tribune*, he has covered welfare reform at the federal and state levels since 1995. From 1991 to 1995 he was an economics correspondent for *U.S. News and World Report* magazine. With Paul Klauda, he is the coauthor of *No Retreat, No Surrender,* an account of the meatpackers' strike at the Hormel Foods Company in 1985.